Cambridge Elements ☰

Elements in Contemporary Performance Texts
edited by
Fintan Walsh
Birkbeck, University of London
Duška Radosavljević
Royal Central School of Speech and Drama, University of London
Caridad Svich
Rutgers University

PERFORMING GRIEF IN PANDEMIC THEATRES

Fintan Walsh
Birkbeck, University of London

CAMBRIDGE
UNIVERSITY PRESS

Shaftesbury Road, Cambridge CB2 8EA, United Kingdom

One Liberty Plaza, 20th Floor, New York, NY 10006, USA

477 Williamstown Road, Port Melbourne, VIC 3207, Australia

314–321, 3rd Floor, Plot 3, Splendor Forum, Jasola District Centre, New Delhi – 110025, India

103 Penang Road, #05–06/07, Visioncrest Commercial, Singapore 238467

Cambridge University Press is part of Cambridge University Press & Assessment, a department of the University of Cambridge.

We share the University's mission to contribute to society through the pursuit of education, learning and research at the highest international levels of excellence.

www.cambridge.org
Information on this title: www.cambridge.org/9781009464819

DOI: 10.1017/9781009464826

First published 2024

A catalogue record for this publication is available from the British Library.

ISBN 978-1-009-46481-9 Hardback
ISBN 978-1-009-46480-2 Paperback
ISSN 2753-2798 (online)
ISSN 2753-278X (print)

Performing Grief in Pandemic Theatres

Elements in Contemporary Performance Texts

DOI: 10.1017/9781009464826
First published online: April 2024

Fintan Walsh
Birkbeck, University of London

Author for correspondence: Fintan Walsh, f.walsh@bbk.ac.uk

Abstract: This Element explores how theatre responded to the death and loss produced by the COVID-19 pandemic, by innovating forms and spaces designed to support us in grief. It considers how theatre grieved for itself, for the dead, for lost ways of living, while also imagining and enacting new modes of being together. Even as it reckoned with its own demise, theatre endeavoured to collectivise grief by performing a range of functions more commonly associated with funerary, health and social care services, which buckled under restrictions and neglect. These pandemic theatres show how grief cannot only be let mourn over individual losses in private, but how it must also seep into the public sphere to fight to save critical services, institutions, communities and art forms, including theatre itself.

This Element also has a video abstract: www.cambridge.org/performing-grief

Keywords: theatre, performance, grief, mourning, pandemic

ISBNs: 9781009464819 (HB), 9781009464802 (PB), 9781009464826 (OC)
ISSNs: 2753-2798 (online), 2753-278X (print)

Contents

'there can be no remaking of the world without ways to allow for our collective sorrow'

Gargi Bhattacharyya, *We, the Heartbroken*

1 Enter Grief: All the World's a Morgue

'We're in a morgue', Tim Crouch announces in *Truth's a Dog Must to a Kennel*, 'All this is dead' (2022: 14). Crouch's one-man performance is an elegy for the theatre that has been mortally wounded by the Covid-19 pandemic, which has devastated the world since the virus was first identified in December 2019. The shutting down of venues, the ending of artistic careers, the decline in audiences, and the rise of digital entertainment are all held up as responsible for the corpse we are invited to view. When I attended the production at Battersea Arts Centre in March 2023, this sense of theatre's mortal risk was amplified by it taking place in the Grand Hall, which was nearly destroyed when fire tore through the space in 2015. Those of us in the theatre, Crouch claims, are like an 'Amazon tribe being buzzed by a microlight' (14), staring up at a digital future that has left us behind. While Crouch laments the death of theatre, he also searches for its redemption among the fragments of a performance of *King Lear*, which he ostensibly views through a VR set, with Shakespeare's play supplying the production's tragic template (Figure 1). However, while Crouch posits digital immersion as theatre's begrudged successor, his own kit doesn't actually work, being only used for effect, and any conjuring is achieved solely via his deft storytelling and our appetite to believe. In this playful conceit, Crouch also lays claim to a stripped-back style of storytelling as one of theatre's most intractable and enduring features. In the end, Crouch subtly disproves his opening claim that what he has to offer is dead, but extends the stark possibility to the audience to consider. As we try to recover from the fallout of the pandemic, Crouch's production asks, what of theatre do we want to keep alive, and what are we willing to pass on as digital simulation or memory?

For Edgar in *King Lear*, who Crouch references, 'the worst is not/ So long as we can say: "This is the worst"' (Shakespeare 2015: 173). While Crouch is being deliberately provocative about theatre's total demise, the mere presence of the audience who have committed to see him indicates that the worst he heralds has, at least, not *yet* come to pass. Certainly, Crouch exaggerates the newness of the threat posed by digital technologies to live theatre, which in fact forms part of a longstanding anxiety that threads throughout the twentieth and twenty-first centuries. But in his strategically histrionic approach, Crouch is as much speaking to us as a theatre worker than as a theatre lover or consumer, whose livelihood is dependent on the popularity of his live art. His task is no longer just to make theatre for a captive audience but to compete against the comforts of streaming television shows, watching films, or gaming at home, which so many of us enjoyed during the pandemic to avoid the risks of entering the public sphere.

Figure 1 Tim Crouch in *Truth's a Dog Must to a Kennel* at Royal Lyceum Theatre, Edinburgh (2022). Courtesy of the photographer Stuart Armitt.

Even if we don't doubt the aliveness of Crouch and his art form, there is some truth to his opening gambit. All may not be dead in this theatrical experience, but we can't deny death's abrupt entry into the centre of our lives since the outbreak of the pandemic. Covid-19 has not just taken approximately 7 million lives through infection but enabled the slow death of careers, organisations, and ways of life. Despite various bailout and support initiatives in some countries, pandemic conditions have affected the theatre industry across the globe's metropolitan centres in particular, resulting in mass redundancies,[1] drops in audience attendance,[2] and funding cuts,[3] while in England they have been used to fuel a long-rumbling attack on arts and humanities subjects led by the

---

[1] In 2020, for instance, the UK entertainment and media union Bectu announced that 5,000 theatre industry workers had lost their jobs due to the effects of coronavirus pandemic. See 'Theatre job losses jump from 3000 to 5000 in a month, reports Bectu' (2020).

[2] In the UK, research gathered by Stage Systems reported a fall in theatre ticket sales throughout the pandemic, from a low of 93 per cent in 2020 to 50 per cent in 2021, with uneven growth reported since. See 'Devastating Impact of the Pandemic on Theatres' (2021). In 2023, the Irish Arts Council announced a significant drop in young people not attending plays, art exhibitions, and other cultural performances, compared to before the pandemic. According to its Director Maureen Kennelly, there was a drop in 16- to 24-year-olds attending Arts Council–supported events, from 64 per cent in 2019 to 52 per cent in 2022. See 'Arts Council warns of "worrying" decline in young people attending events' (2023).

[3] For example, in 2022, Arts Council England announced £50 million a year cuts to London-based arts organisations, as part of its 2023–6 programme, with cuts of approximately 10 per cent expected to be issued by Arts Council of Northern Ireland against affecting arts organisations.

Conservative government.[4] This has all taken place within the context of rising energy prices that make arts venues more challenging to run than before the pandemic, and a cost of living crisis (exacerbated by the Russian invasion of Ukraine in 2022) that limits cultural participation. Despite this hostile backdrop, successive political administrations and organisations around the world have often downplayed or denied the scale of Covid-19, in particular its emotional and psychological fallout, to variously resist culpability, keep the labour market functioning, or peddle distracting conspiracies.

Disappearing Rituals

So woven is death into the historical and conceptual fabric of theatre that denying its presence is impossible. Peggy Phelan has posited that performance and loss are intimately connected – in one sense, live performance is always inclined towards its own disappearance, and in repeating this ritualistically, 'it may well be that theatre and performance respond to a psychic need to rehearse for loss, and especially for death' (1993: 3). According to Herbert Blau, theatrical spectatorship does not only involve reckoning with loss in a philosophical sense, but with the real-time dying of the performer on stage (2011: 114). Early in the pandemic, however, as theatres around the world shut down and the form necessarily evolved digital modes to adapt and survive, artists decided that theatre should not only reckon with death but how to live with loss. As I continue to demonstrate in this text, theatre played a key role in supporting grief in the face of mass death, often by drawing connections between pandemic grief and other losses pertaining to the arts, identity, cultural belonging, work and climate, and the life-sustaining potential of communal gathering via theatre, including digital and live performance. Variously aligning itself with funerary ceremony, health support, and social care, this work tried to respond to the failures of political denial and the collapse of national services under pressure and neglect, drawing on its rich history of striving to make private feelings publicly shared and bearable.

While theatre's resilience and formal agility in evolving digital and distanced modes of communication during the pandemic has been recognised (e.g. Walsh 2021; Fuchs 2022), this text examines its role during and after lockdown periods in responding to an unprecedented scale of grief. Part of theatre's critical innovation during this time, I argue, was to create grief texts and performances to support audiences and communities who struggled to find

---

[4] These include government cuts to subsidies for arts and humanities courses, announced by the Office for Students in 2021, alongside plans to prioritise funding for 'high-value' courses such as STEM and medicine. See 'OfS confirms funding reforms' (2021).

support elsewhere. While I survey the broad cultural landscape, I focus on work emerging from the UK, where I live and experienced the pandemic, and Ireland, where I'm from but couldn't visit, and grieved for in unanticipated ways. As confronting grief requires making room for the ghosts of history, along the way I appeal to fragments of plays and theorists who speak to us from the past to unwittingly guide my understanding of the pandemic and its ongoing effects.

In considering the relationship between theatre and grief, I'm led by a number of questions: how did theatre grieve for itself, for the dead, and for lost ways of living during the Covid-19 pandemic? What new practices and strategies did it evolve to meet legal restrictions, formal limits, and the emotional experiences of its workers, audiences, and those affected? How did theatre step into the support gaps created by political denial and over-pressured health and social care services? What are the potentials and limitations of these adaptations for the future? In asking these questions, my aim is to develop a deeper sense of how these works functioned and what they were striving to intervene in, while also preserving their contributions from the risk of being forgotten. For in facing a post-pandemic future, which is inevitably only an inter-pandemic world, we must not only remember the dead but also the cultural production that helped us make sense of this loss.

Stages of Grief

Grief counsellor and thanatology academic Darcy L. Harris suggests that grief can be a response to loss as well as to death. She defines loss as a condition *'where there is a change in circumstance, perception, or experience where it would be impossible to return to the way things were before'* (2020: 2). This layered model of grief is particularly relevant to the pandemic, in which death and loss intersected on multiple levels globally.

However, a number of features make pandemic grief a distinct phenomenon compared to other experiences of loss. The first owes to its scale, which saw Covid-19 being responsible for millions of deaths worldwide. The second pertains to how this biohazard led to the global destruction of social, leisure, and work life. The third relates to the fact that many political administrations around the world tried to downplay the impact of loss in order to promote economic continuity and disavow responsibility. And finally, successive lockdowns and social distancing mandates meant many people could not engage in public mourning rituals or had to invent new forms to suit the times. With this text, I'm interested in how theatre artists stepped into the void created by the broad absence or inaccessibility of public mourning ceremonies by creating new aesthetic and dramaturgical forms and spaces for grief. In this text, pandemic theatres refer to those practices that supported grief by innovating forms that straddle digital art, installation, film, theatre, performance, and ritual, sometimes drawing on tragic templates and threads. In so doing, they often performed a range of funerary, health, and social care functions when those services buckled under rules or pressure, becoming instrumental lifelines for audiences and communities.

When I suggest that a denial of grief characterised this period, I do not mean to suggest that there was a total lack of awareness of death, loss, and their consequences, but a reluctance to acknowledge and support this publicly in favour of steeling the public to enter battle with the disease. Militaristic language dominated political responses around the world, and it sought to construct an image of strong nations intent on defending their borders against infection and illness. But this rhetorical manoeuvre also functioned to trans-fer the responsibility for social care and healthcare from governments onto the public's willingness to fight, prioritising strength over vulnerability as the path to survival. In the UK, in his coronavirus press conference on 17 March 2020, then Prime Minister Boris Johnson invoked wartime lan-guage to describe the government's strategy:

> We must act like any wartime government and do whatever it takes to support our economy [. . .] Yes this enemy can be deadly, but it is also beatable – and we know how to beat it and we know that if as a country we follow the scientific advice that is now being given we know that we will beat it. And however tough the months ahead we have the resolve and the resources to win the fight. (2020)

A similar tone defined then Irish Taoiseach Leo Varadkar's speech on 12 March 2020 when he appealed: 'I am asking people to make enormous sacrifices. We're doing it for each other. Together, we can slow the virus in its tracks and push it back. Acting together, as one nation, we can save many lives' (Varadkar 2020). Donald Trump, then US President, described himself in a press briefing on 18 March 2020 as a 'wartime President' set on fighting the 'invisible enemy' (Trump in Oprysko and Luthi 2020).[5]

In these instances, the call to fight took precedence over any inclination or invitation to grieve. The broad political denial of grief is reflected in the UK's 2021 House of Commons Health and Social Care, and Science and Technology Committees report, 'Coronavirus: lessons learned to date', which focused on material resources, planning and organisational matters, and not on the

---

[5] Numerous recordings of Trump's live briefing can also be found online. For more on the use of the langue of war in the context of Covid-19, including exceptions to its usage, see Giorgis, P., O. Semenets and B. Todorova (2023), '"We are at war": The military rhetoric of COVID-19 in cross-cultural perspective of discourses'.

emotional and social impact of seismic loss. The subsequent public UK Covid-19 Inquiry has explicitly sought to address the lack of attention given to the experience of grief, with its chair Baroness Heather Hallett expressing a wish to centre the families of the bereaved, including 'the devastating nature of their loss, exacerbated by the impact of the restrictions in place at the time on their ability to grieve' (2022: 8). As Hallett put it in her opening statement: 'The Terms of Reference require the Inquiry to listen to and consider carefully the experiences of bereaved families and others who have suffered hardship or loss as a result of the pandemic' (5).

A report by Lynn Sudbury-Riley and Benito Giordano, 'The Lived Experiences of People Bereaved by Covid-19', highlights the negative impact of mourning rituals being unavailable to people during the pandemic due to rules against public gatherings. Bereavement during Covid-19 differed from other times, the report argues, due to '[r]estrictions on being with family members towards and sometimes at end of life, enduring social isolation whilst newly bereaved, complexity of systems and processes due to lockdown, denial of many important death rituals and strict restrictions on others, negative attitudes among some groups in society, and the ways in which COVID-19 permeates every aspect of life' (2021: 11). This was compounded by 'a lack of available bereavement counselling services, and a particular lack of specialist counselling and mental health services to help people deal with this specific type of grief' (2021: 11). The report continues to champion 'the importance of memorials in bringing some comfort to the bereaved, and the need to ensure COVID-19 victims are not forgotten' (12), underscoring the importance of the National Covid Memorial Wall as an example.

The emerging psychological impact was also addressed by the American Psychiatric Association when announcing that the category of Prolonged Grief Disorder would be added to its revised *DSM-5* (*Diagnostic and Statistical Manual of Mental Disorders*), published in 2022. The condition accounts for intense thoughts of and longing for the deceased most of the day for at least a month, which significantly impair the griever's life. In announcing the addition, the association's President, Vivian B. Pender, highlighted the effect of the pandemic, which 'may make prolonged grief disorder more prevalent' (Pender in American Psychiatric Association 2021). In one sense, the *DSM*'s addition represents a welcome recognition of the scale of grief resulting from the pandemic's scale of loss. In another, however, its inclusion of the qualifier 'prolonged' risks locating the duration as an individual miscalculation, rather than a wholly appropriate response to a still-expanding scale of global loss. If grief is prolonged, it's perhaps only because the pandemic is protracted or because some losses are near impossible to grasp let alone to overcome.

Grief, as Robert A. Neimeyer and Barbara E. Thompson tell us, stands 'at the intersection of attachment and separation, of love and loss' (2014: 3). They propose that the process of grieving is one of '*reaffirming or reconstructing a world of meaning that has been challenged by loss*' (4). I understand grief as an emotional as well as an embodied response to the loss of human life primarily in the context of Covid-19, exacerbated by the simultaneous dismantling of social, cultural, and labour opportunities against a backdrop of climate destruction, often felt most sharply by those at the pandemic's sharp end: the disabled, people of colour, the elderly, LGBTQ+, and working-class people.[6]

The report 'This Too Shall Pass: Mourning collective loss in the time of Covid-19', refers to Covid-19 as 'a crisis of the mind', which strikes at 'the core of how we live as social beings – and also how we die' (2021: 3). Its authors claim that 'the conditions of widespread loss', which characterise the pandemic, render it 'essential that we grieve well', and that this requires us 'doing so collectively, not just on our own' (2021: 3). Part of this requires that we '[i]nvent new rituals and practices to deal with collective loss' (4). This text also argues for the need to collectivise grief and looks to the ways in which theatre developed practices to do so in response to pandemic loss.

While grief may primarily register as an emotional response, experienced as part of a 'crisis of the mind', it also appeals to the dramaturgical practices, aesthetic forms, and ritual patterns of theatre and performance to represent, contain, and support it in order to forge meaningful relationships between what's gone and what remains. According to Therese A. Rando, when grief is expressed as a 'diffuse, global reaction' (1984: 105), it can feel overwhelming. Ritualised practices, in this context, can be used to 'channel feelings of grief into a circumscribed activity having a distinct beginning and ending with a clear purpose, making the feelings more manageable' (105). As Laura S. Lieber puts it, mourning rituals 'channel, contain, and structure otherwise inchoate sensations and emotions; grief rituals and rites integrate one who has experienced a rupture back into the ongoing fabric of community', while '[p]hysical and material expressions of mourning constitute the seams that recognize and sanction discontinuity even as they generate societal coherence' (2016: 101–2). This appeal may be all the more urgent and pressing when grief happens on a large scale and is not recognised. Kenneth Doka uses the term 'disenfranchised grief' to describe

---

[6] For more on how these groups were affected, see the discussions and references in discrete subsequent sections. For data on how the mental health of certain social groups in the UK was affected, see Pierce, M., H. Hope, T. Ford, S. Hatch, M. Hotopf, A. John et al. (2020), 'Mental Health Before and during the COVID-19 Pandemic: A Longitudinal Probability Sample Survey of the UK Population'.

an experience that is not 'openly acknowledged, socially validated, or publicly mourned' (1989: xv). Widespread political denial of pandemic grief forms the backdrop to this text, with theatre and performance stepping in to do the cultural work of recognition, affirmation, and support.

The idea that grief happens in stages was popularised by the psychiatrist Elisabeth Kübler-Ross's *On Death & Dying*. In this book, Kübler-Ross popularised the idea that grief moves through stages, including denial, anger, bargaining, depression, and acceptance (Kübler-Ross 2019 [1969]). Kübler-Ross's model has been taken to mean that grief is progressive and moves through distinct and discrete stages towards closure. What's often omitted from citations of Kübler-Ross's model is that these responses are not fixed and orderly, but also that she developed her ideas from working with the terminally ill who were living (and dying) within a very particular kind of bounded time.

Kübler-Ross's ideas of grief, or certainly their misreading, align with Sigmund Freud's claims that mourning is a process that must be 'overcome' (2001 [1917]: 244) with what he refers to, on a number of occasions, as the 'work of mourning' (245). For Freud, this process is characterised by an acceptance that a love object has gone and is irretrievable, which is the mark of healthy grief. Contrary to this, Freud figures melancholia as a persistent longing for a love object that has already departed, reflecting a refusal to come to terms with loss or to mourn.

Contemporary psychologists and psychiatrists broadly contest these linear or binarised ideas of grief, configuring it as a process that is often unpredictable. Margaret Stroebe and Henk Schut, for instance, challenge the idea that grief can be overcome in linear stages or via a programme of 'grief work', by arguing that grief shuttles and swerves between feelings of loss (focusing on the lost person, yearning, remembering) and restoration (distraction, doing new things, forging new identities and bonds), requiring a much more supple and responsive form of care and attention (1999).

When I refer to stages of grief, I'm not subscribing to an idea of linear recovery that conceives of mourning as a task that can be completed. Nor am I suggesting that the experience of grief can be neatly contained by theatre stages. In many ways, I'm proposing the opposite: that grief is wild and unpredictable; it rises and falls; hides and waits; disappears and suddenly surfaces, requiring new modes of representation to hold and mediate it. As Joan Didion describes it in her memoir about the death of her husband, adapted for the stage in 2007: 'Grief comes in waves, paroxysms, sudden apprehensions that weaken the knees and blind the eyes and obliterate the dailiness of life' (2005: 27). Stages of grief, understood in this context, refer to the forms and spaces of theatrical representation created to hold and support grief. While grief is a response to loss, grief's stages are how theatre responds generatively to that loss, finding forms for who and what remains.

Throughout this text, a number of terms circulate that are distinct but often related: grief, mourning, loss, and absence. Grief is how I account for individual responses to loss – most often death, but also the sudden absence of bodies, ways of being, and cultural practices, in particular theatre. This is not to say that all experiences of loss and absence are met with grief – sometimes grief may not be how we need to respond to loss and absence, and sometimes it might be willfully or affectively denied, suppressed, or in question. Encounters with loss and absence are always haunted by the shadow of grief, especially if the missing object has been valued and loved. In the shadow of mass death, grief chases the heels of absence and loss, regardless of whether or not the lost or absent object is itself being grieved; it may act as a cipher or a stimulus for grief. While grief and mourning are slippery and sometimes interchangeable terms, I tend to prioritise grief. This is largely because in the West, grief is often considered to refer to private feeling and mourning its public expression, which may be overcome by engaging in a process of time-bound, expressive, and codified work.[7] But as I endeavour to establish with this text, lived experiences of grief can challenge established mourning conventions by demanding new cultural forms to support its unique tones and registers, and shifting understandings of what absence, loss, and death mean to those present and living.

Forms for Loss

In exploring theatre's role in supporting pandemic grief, I proceed by making a number of claims. The first is that theatre is an aesthetic practice capable of representing, containing, and supporting grief. While Donald W. Winnicott used the term 'holding' (2005 [1971]: 150) to describe the optimal environment for 'good enough' parenting, theatre might also be seen as a kind of cultural holding space that strives to contain our distress; a transitional object (1975 [1951]) that helps us come to terms with separation, bridging loss, and the unknown world that resides beyond it. Indeed, theatre's tragic roots evidence a foundational belief in the importance of ritualistic practice and communal gathering as a necessary response to suffering.

While theatre's response to grief took on a very particular inflection during the Covid-19 pandemic, it also drew on a long lineage of drama, and in particular tragedy, preoccupied with the dutiful and dignified mourning of the dead, or as Emily R. Wilson has argued, tragedy's preoccupation with 'when it

---

[7] For a useful historical discussion of the relationship between grief and mourning in psychology and psychoanalysis, see Bowlby, J. (1998), *Loss: Sadness and Depression*, pp. 16–18.

is unclear what the future holds or when the end will come' (2004: 5). When Thebes is beset by a mysterious plague in Sophocles's *Oedipus Rex*, for example, the chorus is not only concerned about mounting corpses but by a lack of public mourning: 'generations strewn on the ground/unburied, unwept, the dead spreading death' (1984: 169). Sophocles's *Antigone* pivots on the refusal of King Creon to permit his nephew Polyneices to be grieved, by denying him an official burial. Instead, as Creon puts it: 'a proclamation has forbidden the city/to dignify him with burial, mourn him at all. NO, he must be left unburied, his corpse carrion for birds and dogs to tear, an obscenity for the citizens to behold!' (68). Antigone's denied grief turns to rage, and she insists she will bury her brother, even if she must die to ensure it: 'I have longer to please the dead than please the living here: in the kingdom down below I'll live forever' (63). In *Antigone*, we see how grief, left unbound by recognition and ritual, quickly turns to rage, perhaps best distilled in Anne Carson's question: 'Why does tragedy exist? Because you are full of rage. Why are you full of rage? Because you are full of grief' (2007: 7).

Aristotle teaches us that the emotions of audiences witnessing tragedy may experience the emotional 'purgation' of 'pity and fear' (1907 [1895]: 23), which he refers to as catharsis. The term was popularised by Freud, in developing the talking cure method with Josef Breuer, to account for the emotional and affective discharge that comes with bringing unconscious conflicts to the surface of the mind (2001 [1895]). Others, however, have understood catharsis less as a liberatory practice than as a regulatory function that reinforces the boundaries of good and bad behaviour. The weight of Aristotle's fleeting definition of catharsis has obscured more nuanced readings of tragedy, which in modern and contemporary iterations, including postdramatic forms, are more likely to resonate as a meditation on suffering and grief as a result of social and political conditions, and theatre's capacity to hold us and our pain in recognition and consolation, than as punishment from the Gods. Pandemic theatres both acknowledge this history and extend it, by devising forms that might respond to the unique tragedies of our times.

While an idea prevails in the West, at least, that grief is necessarily private and individual, and mourning is its codified, communal cultural expression, this text's second organising assertion is that theatre demonstrates just how unstable these distinctions can be. Sometimes established mourning practices may hold grief, but sometimes grief overspills both private feeling and the cultural containers available for its expression in a given time and place. In pandemic theatres, we see how grief can pressurise and bypass representational conventions to innovate new forms to hold or mediate its feeling (aesthetic holding and mediation being the same), and also how one grief cannot easily be separated from another, such that a present loss may reactivate a whole history of grief. While theatre does indeed participate in cultural mourning, I'm especially interested in the ways grief frustrates or refuses the call to adhere to available social, cultural, or political conventions, which often assume grief is tidy and time-bound, by creating new forms and outlets for its expression, which in their repetition over time may change what we consider to be acceptable forms of public mourning. In performing grief in pandemic theatres, we are reminded that we have barely begun processing the losses of the Covid-19 pandemic and of the importance of theatre, performance, and artistic practice in this unpredictable and sometimes unending experience.

The third contention is that grief can take the form of an insistence on expressing loss, a refusal to accept it, and a will to commemorate it. Grief, in this context, is caught between three competing relationships to time – present feeling, former idealism, and future possibilities – which play out with varying intensities in theatre and performance. I examine theatre's role in representing, enacting, and staging encounters with grief during the pandemic, as well as the personal, social, and political dimensions of this relationship. Grief often surfaces in this work as an aesthetic concern with light, space, sound, and touch to communicate the interplay of presence and absence, proximity and distance, and a dramaturgical investment in narrative and form to hold grief and commemorate loss. That grief does not and should not solely reside in an individual's interior life is a pivotal principle guiding this this text, argued by demonstrating how loss is mediated at the intersection of aesthetic, personal, social, and political experience. I propose that performing arts, encompassing theatre, performance, music, and installation, are uniquely positioned for relaying and encountering the art of grief, owing to their capacity to render its embodied and relational dimension, and the value of its public experience and expression.

The fourth claim is that one of our most generative responses to grief, and in particular theatre's ability to support us in it, is to ensure the ongoing vitality of the industries that support and sustain it. While theatre has supported us in grief during the pandemic, the pandemic continues to negatively affect theatre's viability owing to funding cuts and dips in audience attendance. To honour the dead requires us to honour theatre, to ensure it retains the capacity to support current and future generations.

Looking Back

In the story of Orpheus and Eurydice, one of western culture's foundational myths, we are reminded that grief, love, and art go hand in hand. Orpheus responded to his grief at the death of his beloved Eurydice with music. Returning to the underworld, playing his lyre to appease Hades and Persephone, Orpheus was permitted to take Eurydice back to the world of the living on the condition that he didn't look back. He does, of course – who wouldn't? – and Eurydice disappears before his eyes. In one version of the myth, he is torn apart by Maenads for his inattention to them, his head left to float down the River Hebrus, still singing mourning songs. Or, as in Jean Cocteau's play *Orphée*, Orpheus begins to disappear before his own eyes when faced with his beloved's loss: 'Eurydice! I can't see my body. I can't find my head' (1961: 38). What the myth of Orpheus teaches us, in its content as well as its recurrence across cultural forms, is that art is one of the most powerful tools we have to both resist and soothe our grief, to hold ourselves intact, while ultimately helping us to draw a functional, if provisional, boundary between the worlds of the living and dead, what is lost and what remains. This text, and the work discussed within it, similarly draw us into the underworld of grief, while also steering us towards a safer surface.

While this section introduces the context of pandemic grief and its relationship to theatre, subsequent sections focus on discrete forms and shades of grief. Section 2 explores how theatre responded to its own (near) demise during the pandemic, with live-streamed and digital productions that presented theatres as dying or dead, inviting viewers to grieve over its remains – the variously half-lit, dark, empty, silent, haunted, or partitioned venues left behind. Grieving for theatre and live performance involved observing their absorption into the digital realm, where we were often invited to ask if this was an act of rescue and preservation or ruin? I explore how a number of productions mourned the loss of live theatre via absent stages and auditoria, while compelling us to ask more complex philosophical questions, such as what is theatre without an audience, and what is an audience without a performer or performance? Among the works addressed include Hester Stefan Chillingworth's *Caretaker* (2020), which was live-streamed on YouTube from the empty Jerwood Theatre Downstairs at the Royal Court Theatre, London; Daniel Kitson's *Dot.Dot.Dot.* (2020), in which the performer reflected on the pandemic to an empty auditorium in London's Union Chapel; Dead Centre's *To Be A Machine (Version 1.0)*, which was initially live-streamed from an audience-free Project Arts Centre, Dublin in 2020; Lost Dog's *In a Nutshell* (2020), in which mediatised memories of a recently obliterated theatre filled an otherwise empty auditorium in the Connaught Theatre, Worthing; and National Theatre of Scotland's theatre film *Ghost Light* (2020), which replayed moments in Scottish theatre history in the wake of theatrical closure.

Section 3 explores productions created to remember the bereaved and the dead, stepping into roles normally reserved for faith-based institutions and state services. While sketching the broader landscape of cultural commemoration, it takes as its focus a selection of digital and in-person performances, including Talawa

Theatre's *Tales from the Front Line ... and other stories* (2020–1), Taryn Simon's *An Occupation of Loss: Laments from Quarantine* (2020), Tara Theatre's audio-walk *Farewell* (2021), and Jo Clifford and Lesley Orr's memorial service *The Covid Requiem* (2021). Exploring how these forms worked to remember and commemorate the dead, in particular for some of the most marginalised and affected communities, I consider how theatre performed the unofficial function of striving to locate the pandemic experience in a longer history of grief – experiences which have preceded it and those inevitably yet to come.

With Section 4, I examine productions that advanced new forms of assembly as central to the processing of grief by rendering it as socially and culturally necessary. Identifying the wave of Black Lives Matter protests which erupted around the world as a pivotal moment when injustice and grief intersected to insist on the need for new forms for public assembly, it focuses on work that questions the relationship between digital and in-person assembly, while also stressing the need for new forms of gathering to respond to issues of cultural, social, political, and ecological urgency. Among the work considered includes Nina Segal's *Assembly* (2021), which queried how humans might come together to respond to the social and ecological fallout of the pandemic; Dante or Die's *Skin Hunger* (2020) and Fevered Sleep's *8 Tender Solitudes* (2021), which explored the need for human touch in the wake of the pandemic; the Belfast Ensemble's *MASS* (2021), which posited immersive opera as a form of secular group worship, including for the queer artists whose images are projected around it; and THISISPOPBABY'S *WAKE* (2022), which enacted a jubilant Irish wake to respond to the pandemic. I track how these productions mourn and commemorate our losses, but also orient us towards imagining and participating in new forms of cultural, social, and political assembly premised on recognising shared experiences of loss.

While celebrating theatrical culture's adaptability under these conditions, this text ultimately challenges political moves to leave this important and incomplete work to the arts alone, not least while governments simultaneously underfund and denigrate them. The best way to honour these pandemic theatres of grief, I conclude, is to ensure that the vibrancy and versatility of the theatre presented during the pandemic – indeed, in spite of it – are adequately supported and built on in the future, which includes maintaining a cultural archive of grief that we may call on when we will inevitably need to again.

2 Who's There?: Theatre Mourns Itself

At least since Bernardo first shouted into the auditorium at the start of *Hamlet*, 'Who's there' (Shakespeare 1992: 1), theatre has never been sure of who or what is really absent or present, alive or dead. As we sat in front of screens to watch digital theatre during the pandemic, Bernardo's call became 'Can you see me? Can you hear me?' as performers and audiences alike doubted the existence of each other. Shakespeare's audiences were no strangers to the effects of plague either, due to the bubonic plague's devastating effects across Europe since the fourteenth century, ending with the Great Plague of London in 1665–6, which may even have been responsible for the death of Shakespeare's son Hamnet.[8] During the Covid-19 pandemic, theatre had to confront this uncertainty of who was present or absent, alive or dead, in very real ways too, owing to the loss of life as well as the compulsory closure of theatres, which killed off some companies and careers for good. For Crouch, as we saw in the previous section, theatre became a morgue unto itself. Here, I depart from Crouch's claim to focus on the range of ways that theatre responded to its own brush with death – temporary, expected, or lasting – with digital productions that presented theatres as dying or dead, inviting viewers to grieve over its remains; the variously half-lit, dark, empty, silent, and haunted venues left behind. I explore how a number of productions mourned the loss of theatre via absent stages and auditoria, while compelling us to ask: what is theatre without an audience, and what is an audience without a performer or performance? Among the works discussed include Hester Stefan Chillingworth's installation *Caretaker* (2020), live-streamed on YouTube from the Royal Court Theatre's Jerwood Theatre Downstairs; Daniel Kitson's *Dot.Dot.Dot.* (2020), live-streamed from Union Chapel, London; Dead Centre's *To Be A Machine (Version 1.0)* (2020), live-streamed from Project Arts Centre, Dublin; Lost Dog's *In a Nutshell* (2020), live-streamed on YouTube from the Connaught Theatre, Worthing, by The Place, London; and National Theatre of Scotland's theatre film *Ghost Light* (2020), which replayed moments in Scottish theatre history. Mired in grief, this theatre quivered affectively and narratively between remembrance and imminence, reckoning with what's been lost and what might emerge again.

Grief is often perceived to be an individual's response to loss, felt at a psychic and bodily level, but the effect of the pandemic on theatre also produced a kind of cultural grieving within the theatre industry for itself. In the case of theatre productions grieving the loss of live performances, buildings, workers, and audiences, this was typically communicated via darkened stages, empty spaces, long stretches of silence, or fragmented narratives straining to be heard, and the structural encounter with the vivid but impermeable digital screen. These aesthetic choices communicated that something of theatre had been lost, while also inviting us to search for what remained amid its material ruins and

---

[8] While the cause of Hamnet's death at eleven years old is unknown, many assume it was due to the bubonic plague. This is the reason supplied by Maggie O'Farrell in her novel *Hamnet* (2020), and its subsequent stage adaption in 2023 by Lolita Chakrabarti for the Royal Shakespeare Company.

digital reconstructions. While demonstrating how these works served as grief practices, I also propose that they pressured us to reconsider established beliefs in theatre and performance studies regarding the relationship between presence and absence, (a)liveness, and death.

Lying in State

Hester Stefan Chillingworth's *Caretaker* took place between May and October 2020. A durational installation, *Caretaker*, involved the live-streaming of the empty Jerwood Theatre Downstairs at London's Royal Court Theatre, whose set was designed by Chloe Lamford for Vicky Featherstone's production of E.V. Crowe's *Shoe Lady* that was playing when the theatre shut down due to compulsory closure orders (Figure 2). In the course of the live stream, the theatre's dim light slowly changed states, and the installation was accompanied by messages, which Chillingworth penned almost daily to respond to current news events and their sense of the world. 'As in any theatre, you are not really alone when you experience *Caretaker*' (17 May 2020), one post stated, and in the wake of the murder of George Floyd under police chokehold in Minneapolis, Minnesota on 25 May 2020, one comment drew a distinction between grief for theatre and grief for human life: 'Don't be silent about the murder of George Floyd. Or the horrendous Trump calling the protestors thugs. Or the fact that we are no better and no less racist in the UK.

Figure 2 *Caretaker*, live-streamed on YouTube from the Royal Court Theatre's Jerwood Theatre Downstairs, London (2020). Courtesy of the Royal Court Theatre.

Don't be silent. Please make noise. On this, silence equals complicity. On this, silence equals death. Know when to be silent. And know when to make noise' (30 May 2020).

Chillingworth describes *Caretaker* as their response to 'the need, a desire, a yearning for the voice of theatre not to fall silent' (2020). Their hope was that the installation offered 'a space of respite, contemplation and recharge [. . .] a sort of secular sanctuary, not just for people from the theatre industry but from anywhere' (2020). In watching an empty stage, Chillingworth wished to remind audiences that 'the world is still there', while activating their appetite for 'new ways of watching performance' (2020). Chillingworth's rationale strikes a rather upbeat note – in their view, *Caretaker* is about the assurances of emptiness and silence, the pleasure of quiet potential. The title, in Chillingworth's explanation, emphasises the artwork's capacity to care for audiences while we wait for theatre to return, but the production is structured around nurturing the audience's care for theatre during its closure.

My own experience of *Caretaker* was that it communicated less a sense of care than repose, produced by turning the theatre into a kind of hospital, church, morgue, or graveside that we were invited to grieve over. My immediate response was that it resembled those hospital TV channels that allow patients to view the facility's mostly empty churches at any time of the day or night. In particular, *Caretaker* reminded me of all the funeral services I attended online during the pandemic as a result of restrictions imposed by pandemic legislation on public gatherings, in which screens became almost voyeuristic portals into the grief of those few permitted to gather in person. But the open trap door, centre stage, also evoked a graveside scene, including the gravedigging scene in *Hamlet*. We are not here to bury Ophelia or exhume Yorick, however, but to attend theatre's own burial.

Chillingworth's installation appears to respond to the opening gambit of Peter Brook's *The Empty Space*, in which he writes: 'A man walks across this empty space whilst someone else is watching him, and this is all that is needed for an act of theatre to be engaged' (1996 [1968]: 7). In Brook's formulation, all that's required for theatre to exist is one person viewing another in shared space, contrary to what happens in the cinema, which at the time of his book's writing, was deemed to be theatre's gravest threat. In Chillingworth's installation, however, the space without bodies is neither theatre nor pure emptiness, but somewhere in between – a suspensive site of history, absence, and possibility. Certainly, Chillingworth's artwork is an installation, but its intervention into the pandemic asks us to view theatre not only as bodily co-presence in shared space but also as the audience's digital co-remembrance and anticipation of theatrical activity, and the theatre's evidencing of its own enduring history as an invitation to wait in hope.

A Performer in Search of an Audience

While *Caretaker*'s elegiac form is anchored in the total absence of human bodies from the theatre space, turning the theatre into a sickbed, morgue, or graveside that we are invited to watch over, in Daniel Kitson's *Dot.Dot.Dot.* the writer and performer takes centre stage in an empty theatre, as if searching for the audience that has abandoned him. Set in London's Union Chapel, Kitson sits behind a small table, with an empty auditorium stretching out behind him. As the live stream begins, a wide-angle shot of the stage from the back of the auditorium captures Kitson pottering around the stage, his back mostly to the screen audience. An overhead shot reveals he is arranging items on a small table (Figure 3), pitched in front of a large pulpit, as music by Sault and Jerry Lewis plays around him. This continues for a little over one hour, evoking a sense of the unrushed mundanity of everyday life during the pandemic, with the performer evidencing little interest in us seeing him or he seeing us.

When Kitson eventually sits down to face the camera, he explains how he has been recording the events, people, and insights from his own pandemic experience. 'I've got 186 post-it notes to show you', he tells us, 'and 74 photographs'. Kitson's performance unfolds as he picks up his photographic evidence and post-its on the table and uses them as prompts to document his pandemic experience. At one point, he stresses that while the pandemic is 'devastating', it's also 'doing something'. 'It's exposing entrenched inequities, ways that can no longer be ignored', he claims. 'It's highlighting the need for open spaces,

Figure 3 Daniel Kitson in *Dot.Dot.Dot.* (2020) at Union Chapel, London. (Live stream screengrab.)

access rights.' While his own observations and recollections feature deaths, they are dominated by recounting births, separations, reunions, not washing, baking, and eating. He wasn't especially keen to write about the pandemic, he confesses, but 'writing about anything other than what's happening right now feels like eating a Viennetta in a tornado'. In the confidence of Kitson's address, relative to the absence that surrounds him, the production plays into the tension between denial and acceptance that characterised responses to the pandemic, in particular as it affected theatre.

This production concerns the scale of destruction engendered by the pandemic and how it affected Kitson personally, as well as the cultural industries in which he participates. While Kitson recognises this loss via the empty theatre that encircles him and in his anecdotes, the production foremost focuses on his response to loss, especially his coping strategies. The ordinary tasks, which recur throughout Kitson's performance, point to the rituals that hold together everyday life, while the post-its and photographs are the dramaturgical devices deployed to organise diffuse experience, as well as the performance we witness digitally.

Kitson also senses that reckoning with prior loss involves preparation for future loss. His friends are moving out of the London city that they once shared and he loves, he tells us, but he fears their departure more than he fears an empty theatre: 'I want my friends to be happy and I want my friends to be safe, but it feels like the cities I love are emptying themselves of the people that make me love them. And I found myself picturing a moment in the future when I will stand in these places and miss those people.'

The performance by Kitson is neither as melancholic nor as austere as Chillingworth's installation in terms of its comment on how the pandemic has affected theatre. In the opening minutes, Kitson acknowledges the grandeur of the space around him while also suggesting that his performance does not depend on it to exist. 'What a magnificent space', he remarks, 'I'm not going to be using any of that bit'. Nonetheless, in relaying his starting point for the show, Kitson shares his wish to tour around empty theatres while streaming his performance to a limited capacity that matches that of the venue in question. In this ambition, Kitson's project is less a meditation on the death of theatre, as in Chillingworth's installation, than an experiment in the material absence of the audience and his shifting attitude towards their loss and digital displacement, as well as an investigation into whether or not theatrical scale and proximity can be replicated online. 'I know that you are there and I am here', he says to the camera, but his sense of our real *thereness* remains ambiguous.

Union Chapel is a functioning church, entertainment venue, and drop-in centre for the homeless in Islington, London. Performance in this building is inevitably imbued with a sense of religious ceremony, which underscores the funerary dimension of Kitson's project. A couple of months prior to *Dot.Dot.Dot.* taking place, Max Porter read his novel *Grief is the Thing With Feathers* from the same stage in a similarly empty theatre, streamed to audiences to raise funds for their homelessness charity. 'Moving on, as a concept, is for stupid people', Porter's bereaved Dad says, 'because any sensible person knows grief is a long-term project. I refuse to rush' (2015: 99). While Porter's novel was published pre-pandemic in 2015 and concerns the effect of a woman's death on her two sons and husband, the sense that grief requires both secular and religious responses to sustain us through it was amplified by its recitation in Union Chapel.

While Kitson's dramaturgy is structured around remembering his experience of the pandemic, in its brisk rhythm and often matter-of-fact tone, it resists being stuck in that past. In the closing moments, Kitson speaks to the camera: 'I believe the most heart-breaking thing about being alive is also the most hopeful thing about being alive, which is the fact that everything that happens, *everything* that happens, is eventually a thing that happened a very long time ago.' Even though Kitson's production is about personal and cultural loss during the pandemic, he concludes by telling us that his is not just a project of circular wallowing or exhumation, but of rhythmically and ritualistically assigning this experience to the past.

A Mind in Search of a Body

In querying the presence of a remote audience, Kitson echoes the concern of Dead Centre's mediatised production, *To Be A Machine (Version 1.0)*, which was initially presented as part of the Dublin Theatre Festival in October 2020. Directed by Bush Moukarzel and Ben Kidd for Dublin-based Dead Centre, the production was based on Mark O'Connell's 2017 collection of essays on transhumanism, a movement of those who desire to escape their bodies in favour of a technologically enhanced form. In this production, Mark is played by actor Jack Gleeson, who delivers his performance live but effectively alone in the black box theatre of Project Arts Centre, Dublin, which I viewed on my laptop at home in London. Those of us viewing online submitted brief video recordings of our faces before the show, which were then displayed on iPads in the otherwise empty theatre, so that both Mark and the audience are forced to encounter our simultaneous absence and presence; to confront the loss of live performance in favour of digital transposition (Figure 4). Like the transhumanists of O'Connell's book, both the performer and audience have uploaded our data, so that we might extend the boundaries of our bodies under quarantine to come together and grieve all that we have lost, in particular our shared experience of theatre.

Figure 4 Jack Gleeson as Mark in *To Be a Machine (Version 1.0)* at Protect Arts Centre, Dublin, 2020. Photograph by Ste Murray. Courtesy of Dead Centre.

This uncanny theatre of faces floating on iPads is both strange and common – strange for theatre but ubiquitous in terms of how we now communicate on smart phones, computers and tables, and increasingly so during the pandemic.[9] These screens also set up a comparison between the kind of data uploading we have done for this performance with the work of Alcor cryogenics lab, Arizona, which O'Connell visits as part of his research. Alcor describes itself as concerned with 'preserving life by pausing the dying process using subfreezing temperatures with the intent of restoring good health with medical technology in the future'.[10] In his book, O'Connell relays that procedures often involve the decapitation and storage of heads, until such a time as technology might be able to revitalise them. At one point during the performance, a camera slowly pans across the audience with our eyes now closed (using the 'sleeping' video viewers have uploaded), as O'Connell's description of the Alcor labs is given to draw parallels with our own condition:

---

[9] Data sets suggest that 2020 experienced a significant spike in internet usage around the world, with the use of video-calling applications doubling in the UK. For example, see *Online Nation: 2020 Summary report* (2020), p. 11.

[10] See Alcor website.

> Surrounded by the severed heads of technoutopians, I thought of the Catholic concept of limbo, a place that was neither heaven nor hell, but a state of suspension, a holding pattern for the souls of the righteous who had died before they could be properly redeemed by the coming of Christ. These patient souls were being held in a state of hopeful deferral, until the future came to deliver them from their own deaths.

As the digital audience is invited to view our displaced heads mounted on iPads, as in a cryogenics lab, we are steered to consider transhumanists as engaged in a grotesque form of death disavowal, while questioning whether or not this mediatised theatre represents an expansion of form, or an equally disturbing zone of death denial and grief deferral.

While he addresses the audience via a camera, Mark still doubts our existence. He generates chat boxes within our viewing screens to ask us how we think we will die. The (scripted) reply 'alone', he claims, is a distinctly human answer, whereas a machine would likely supply a condition. A failure to quickly provide an answer to a math problem, he concludes, confirms the existence of a human audience, as a machine would answer this instantly. 'Are you enjoying the show?', Mark asks at one point, before following up with, 'You are still there, aren't you?' Mark needs assurance that someone, or something, is with him; that he is not an actor without an audience. The problem here is not so much whether or not machines think, but rather does the audience exist, and if so, how do we know? In this, Mark reminds us of many Beckettian characters who decide to go on even when meaning has lapsed. Trapped inside the black box studio, in particular, he evokes Winnie in Beckett's *Happy Days*, who isn't sure if her husband Willy, who is hidden behind the mound of earth that engulfs her, is alive or dead. Like Mark, Winnie sidesteps her anxieties by assuming life goes on even in the face of death: 'There always remains something. (Pause.) Of everything. (Pause.) Some remains. (Pause.)' (2010 [1961]: 30).

In *To Be a Machine*, our existence as an audience ultimately cannot be assumed through language but needs to be confirmed by touch, as we will revisit in Section 4. At one point, Mark tries to hug an audience member on an iPad, his body awkwardly straining around its rigid contours. We grieve not just for the dead and the absent but also for live performance's capacity to support our grief via physical proximity to others.

An Audience in Search of a Theatre

While Kitson and Gleeson occupy stages in empty theatres, in Lost Dog's *In a Nutshell*, performer Ben Duke sits in an otherwise empty auditorium of red chairs, looking directly at the camera. 'Hello my name is Ben Duke', the

Figure 5 Ben Duke in *In a Nutshell* (2020), the Connaught Theatre, Worthing. (YouTube screengrab.)

performer begins, 'I'm a choreographer and a performer, rather I *was* a choreographer and a performer, and I've been asked to create this short film about the experience of theatre' (Figure 5). With this, Duke switches into past tense, to describe what theatre *used* to be like, like a guide at an archaeological site delivering a eulogy or reconstructing history from ruins. Unlike *Caretaker* and *Dot.Dot.Dot.*, in which a return to life still seems possible for theatre, *In a Nutshell* proceeds from the basis that theatre is firmly dead, consigned to the past, and exists now only as fragments of memory.

'The stage is a magical place where all kinds of things can happen', Duke tells us, before recalling moments in former productions. He begins with the preponderance of *Hamlet*, the one with the Argentinians, the image of a dead baby's body presented on a shield (Euripides's *The Trojan Women*), Poseidon. The memory of a woman in a 'terrible rage' recalls Mrs J in Caryl Churchill's pre-apocalyptic *Escaped Alone*, who breaks from the play's cosy backyard realism to incant in the dark:

> Terrible rage terrible rage terrible rage terrible
> rage terrible rage terrible rage terrible rage terrible
> rage terrible rage terrible rage terrible rage terrible
> rage terrible rage terrible rage terrible rage terrible
> rage terrible rage terrible rage terrible rage terrible
> rage terrible rage terrible rage terrible rage terrible
> rage terrible rage. (2019 [2016]: 179)

As the Chorus Leader knows in Euripides's *The Trojan Women*, 'Only tears can soothe the afflicted, tears/And dirges sung to the melodies of grief' (2009: 52).

These recollections are punctuated by Duke occasionally staring blankly ahead or turning his head to the side, as if straining to access a memory. In these pensive, wistful interludes, the production emphasises that there are aspects of this ancient practice called theatre that are now beyond reach, and via this digital technique, reminds us of theatre's unique investment in shared space-time experiences.

In recalling moments from the theatre, what strikes Duke the most is the power of audience proximity. Sometimes, other audience members' legs rested against you in the auditorium, he recalls, advising viewers to try it with someone at home or with a pet or plant. There is no guarantee, after all, that any of us are left with human company. Duke is speaking in a world where physical proximity has become such a remote concept that we need to rehearse it. Theatre was, in many ways, a hassle, he tells us, but in a packed auditorium, audiences both hemmed you in and held you. When the lights went down in the theatre, Duke informs us, the audience 'kind of vanish but are still there'. Here, theatrical experience and its remembrance are intertwined. As Louise Owen and Marilena Zaroulia write of the production: 'We recall nights in the theatre via fragments of memory and incomplete associations; sometimes, these very particular experiences and ways of making sense of a piece of performance cannot be disentangled from the memory of the actual work' (2022: 212).

He once sat so close to the action that he could have thrown a shoe at Poseidon, Duke recounts, while the visibility of a performer's sweat patches confirmed that she was 'real' and 'going through something . . . we're going through something together'. Addressing the screen audience, whom he can't see, Duke claims that it had 'three dimensionality', unlike us – 'you're not real to me'. In the experience of watching the dead baby on stage, Duke recalls 'the softness of death' – how it looked and felt in shared space, and how this feeling palpably passed throughout the auditorium. He is much more doubtful of his exchange with the digital viewer, concluding the piece with: 'You're probably not there.'

The production's tragic investments are revealed in allusions to *Hamlet*, whose character is defined by Claudius as 'unmanly grief' (Shakespeare 1992: 9) in the wake of his father's death. As well as the explicit opening reference, the title comes from Act Two, Scene Two, when Hamlet responds to Rosencrantz's accusation that he is too ambitious: 'O God, I could be bounded in a nut shell and count myself a king of infinite space were it not that I have bad dreams' (40). With this, Hamlet denies his own ambition by expressing a preference for living in his head instead of the world, a reality that would be possible if it were not for the dreams that disrupt his thinking. There is a suggestion here that Duke's bounded world, implicitly bolstered to keep the pandemic outside, is both a space of infinite imagination as well as one vulnerable to repressed, forgotten, and partially remembered experiences.

Another tragic intertext is Homeric accounts of the Trojan War. These emerge in the image of Poseidon carrying the trident, in the spare musical backing of Henry Purcell's opera *Dido and Aeneas*, and in the allusion to the camera as being 'like a Cyclops'. In the myth, Odysseus blinds Cyclops to make his way home from Troy, only to be punished by the Gods. In his engagement with the camera, Duke tacitly presents himself as an Odysseus figure who reckons with the camera to try and make his way home, which in this digital presentation, viewed on laptops and iPads, includes making his way into our homes and inviting us into his (lost) theatre.

A Theatre Summons Its Ghosts

While the productions discussed so far have explored different kinds of grief in response to loss – of theatres, of performers, of the audience – National Theatre of Scotland's film *Ghostlight*, directed by Hope Leach, fully embraces its ghosts as not yet fully dead. Conceived in collaboration with National Theatre of Scotland director Jackie Wylie and former Traverse Theatre director Philip Howard for the Edinburgh International Film Festival, the work is not just interested in theatre's most visible workers, such as actors, but its invisible crew – those backstage, in wardrobe, rehearsing, or lingering in the wings. As a production for a national theatre, it also mourns the loss of theatre for a nation by reminding us of its role in cultural construction and questioning, and implicitly advocating that we fight for it to continue.

Even though the National Theatre of Scotland is an entity without its own building, the production was filmed at the Festival Theatre in Edinburgh. At the time of making, this theatre, like many around the world, was in the dark, with only a ghost light indicating a glimmer of life. A ghost light refers to a light kept on in theatres while it's empty or closed, and its main purpose is for safe access for theatre workers during darkness. But during the pandemic, many theatres around the world declared keeping their ghost lights on as a sign of their commitment to return. The practice inspired a number of digital productions, including Western Australian Opera's *Ghostlight Opera* (2020). Finland's National Theatre presented the installation *Ghost Light* (2020), created by Mark Niksanaen and Jani Martti-Salo in collaboration with Inkeri Aula. Filmed on the Small Stage of the National Theatre, we see a standing light centre stage surrounded by a disembodied voice that meditates on it being empty, the natural world, pollution, and the interconnection of the planet's ecosystems. As the voice speaks, the light pulsates as if thought and light are one. 'It's quite relaxing when there's nobody here', it muses, finding perspective on the theatre's closure in light of global environmental concerns.

Unlike either of these artworks, the National Theatre of Scotland foregrounds its ghosts more than its darkened light. As the camera moves around the building, its light flickering between obscurity and full illumination, it reveals spectres from the theatre's rich past: snippets of productions, rehearsed readings, backstage labour. Among those featured include James McArdle performing as Rona Munro's James I in *The James Plays* (2014), Anna Russell Martin in Jenni Fagan's *The Panopticon* (2019), and Siobhan Redmond standing in the wings reciting a poem about the theatre by poet Jackie Kay.

The film draws to a close with the noise of an audience gathering, sounding somewhere between memory and imminent possibility. While the other productions explored in this section approached theatre as mortally wounded or dead, this production opened with a scene from David Grieg's 2010 stage version of J. M. Barrie's *Peter Pan*, a work steeped in the (im)possibility of life everlasting. With this opening and the flood of ghosts that followed it, the National Theatre of Scotland appeared not quite ready to announce the death of theatre or to let its ghost rest, but to encourage viewers, like its makers, to at least believe, however foolishly, in its eternal life.

Philip Auslander has proposed that liveness is not the exclusive domain of direct performer–audience interactions, but that it can also refer to 'a sense of always being connected to other people, of continuous, technologically mediated temporal co-presence with others known and unknown' (2012: 6). Liveness, Auslander tells us, does not belong to the object, its effect or mediation, but pertains to 'an interaction produced through our engagement with the object and our willingness to accept its claim' (9). While the digital works explored in this section show theatre workers grieving over live performance, by allowing its screened mediation to appear like a window into a critically injured or departed form, they simultaneously provoke our willingness to believe that liveness persists; that something of theatre lives on.

During the pandemic, theatre responded to its own near-death by evolving digital forms that invited audiences to grieve over its remains. From the empty theatre of *Caretaker* to the vacant auditoria of *Dot.Dot.Dot.* and *To Be a Machine*, to the invisible stage of *In a Nutshell* and the spectral visions of *Ghost Light*, theatre asserted its resilience and capacity to innovate, even as it lamented the loss of its former incarnation. Simultaneously, these productions also grappled with philosophical questions about theatre foregrounded by the experience of pandemic loss: can theatre exist without a body? Can it live with one performer or a single audience member? Is a belief in theatre's ghosts enough to bring it back to life? Or, to paraphrase Gertrude's response to Hamlet claiming he saw his father's ghost, are these 'bodily creation[s]' (1992: 76) temporary chimeras that both represent and conceal all that has been lost but cannot yet be fully accepted? While these difficult questions are left to linger rather than be answered, and will undoubtedly preoccupy theatre and perform-ance studies for years to come, collectively the productions staged theatre's losses, drawing on its formal and historical preoccupation with absence and death. But an empty stage is always one that has been vacated as well as one that is waiting to be filled, and even in the darkest, quietest, barest space, this work also thrummed with the potential for theatrical life to return.

3 To Name the Names: Commemorating the Dead

An explosion of red hearts hangs over London's River Thames, swelling along the walls of London's South Bank, opposite the Palace of Westminster. Begun in March 2021, this National Covid Memorial Wall mural was created by volunteers and managed by the Covid-19 Bereaved Families for Justice campaign to record each life lost due to the virus (Figure 6). In the face of the often-blithe datafication of death, which saw lives reduced to numbers in news reports, the project was spurred by the wish for each hand-painted heart to identify, record, and remember individuals who died. Similar initiatives to commemorate the dead took place around the world, including the planting of a Forest of Memory in Bergamo, Italy; the tying of blue and white ribbons to

Figure 6 A section of the National Covid Memorial Wall, London, 2021. Photograph by Kelly Foster. Courtesy of Wikipedia Commons.

St. James Presbyterian Church in Bedford Gardens, east of Johannesburg; the planting of white flags by activists outside Brazil's Congress; Suzanne Brennan Firstenberg's temporary art installation, 'In America: Remember', next to the Washington Monument, consisting of thousands of white flags; and the Pandemic Heroes Monument in Bandung, Indonesia. In different ways, each of these public monuments and artworks sought to remember the dead by presenting us with a visual representation and reminder of the sheer scale of loss endured.

While the National Covid Memorial Wall is a particularly striking visual monument to pandemic grief, its guiding impulse has also been shared by theatre and performance artists. As discussed in the previous section, while a swathe of work mourned the (near) death of theatre, other productions sought to identify and remember individual lives, stepping into roles normally reserved for faith-based institutions and state services. This section focuses on a selection of these works, which took place both online and in-person, including Talawa Theatre's *Tales from the Front Line ... and other stories* (2020–1), Taryn Simon's *An Occupation of Loss: Laments from Quarantine* (2020), Tara Theatre's audio-walk *Farewell* (2021), and Jo Clifford and Lesley Orr's memorial service *The Covid Requiem* (2021). Exploring how these forms worked to remember the dead, in particular for some of the most marginalised and affected communities, the section considers how theatre attempted to document and understand the losses of the present for future generations to understand.

Judith Butler has explored which lives are grievable, arguing that the life deemed to be worthy of grief is the life that matters (2009). 'Without grievability', Butler tells us, 'there is no life, or, rather, there is something living that is other than life' (15). While Butler writes about the conditions of war in particular, her writing has broader implications in demonstrating how political and cultural conventions and practices – enacted and withheld – have the capacity to cast some lives as ungrievable and therefore as lives that do not count. When grief is foreclosed, the life that has been lived goes unvalued, and when grief is forcibly denied, the dead are figured as disposable. During the pandemic, as governments around the world tried to downplay the emotional fallout of the loss of life, they were no doubt, in part, trying to protect citizens from the shocking scale of human death, but also concealing their own failures by casting those ungrieved as lives that did not matter.

The broad denial of grief, which I position this work as reacting against, is informed by a defence against political and social culpability, and its underlying shame, and the shame of public grieving as an admission of loss and even responsibility. Michael Cholbi suggests that grief has been philosophically eschewed, likely because it has been considered to be 'a source of shame'

(2021: 6). Shame, Fred Cooper, Luna Dolezal, and Arthur Rose tell us, operated as a powerful policing affect during the pandemic, directed at categorising the 'morally worthy and unworthy' in terms of those who deserved care and protection and those who endangered others, often 'at the expense of the vulnerable and the marginalized' (2023: 2). To grieve the dead via performance requires not only public expression but also a wilful resistance against the shame that suppresses such actions and their political and social implications.

A recurring feature of these works is the use of sound, voice, and music to support the public grieving of the dead and the occupation of public space, including outdoors. Sound, in the works explored in this section, holds and communicates memory and feeling, circulating vibrationally between the public and private spheres; in and between spaces and bodies. As David J. Roy tells us, we 'turn to music to carry mourning too heavy for words and preaching', a reminder that 'all indeed is never lost, that some blessings are unburiable' (2001: 132). As a social practice, listening to music and organised sound helps us feel connected with 'a community of other mourners' (Stein 2004: 808). But this performance of grief, as I continue to track here, is inseparable from an affirmation not only of liveness, as in the last section, but of still being alive.

Grief Workers

Based in South London, Talawa Theatre interviewed Black workers in schools, rail, and healthcare settings and used their testimonies to produce a six-part series of short films, *Tales from the Front Line … and other stories*. Black and ethnic minority staff represented a disproportionate share of frontline and key workers during the pandemic, rendering them more vulnerable to illness as they supported public services.[11] Created during lockdowns between August 2020 and February 2021, the films reflect on the impact of the pandemic on the workers' experiences, focusing on how they navigated public responsibility and private grief. Couched within this leading narrative thread is a persistent longing by those interviewed for art, music, movement, and touch to salve their losses, which public assembly, theatre and performance once enabled. These films offer themselves as substitutes to co-present theatrical contact while leaving us with the question of whether or not this digital representation is a sufficient replacement for the kinds of communal gatherings mourned in the films.

---

[11] Black and minority ethnic individuals represented a disproportionately large share of key workers in health, social care, food supply, and utility sectors during the pandemic, in particular, in London. See 'Black and minority ethnic workers make up a disproportionately large share of key worker sectors in London', The Health Foundation (2020).

Directed by the company's artistic director, Michael Buffong, in the film *The Teacher* an educator (Jo Martin) speaks directly to the camera from inside a school about trying to keep students safe during the pandemic, against a backdrop of poor communication from the government and budgetary cuts (Figure 7). During the same period, the murder of George Floyd and the response of the Black Lives Matter movement went off 'like an explosion' in the teacher's head, she tells us, who realised she was 'angry all the time'. The teacher's address to the camera is dreamily intercut with scenes of performers Rhys Dennis and Waddah Sinada (of FUBUNATION) dancing outside the school, their yearning gestures conveying a longing for closeness, while also confounding stereotypes of Black masculinity as aggressive and violent (Figure 8). The interlude is drawn from the performers' multidisciplinary series *Ruins*, which premiered in 2019 with the aim of exploring the effects of intergenerational trauma on marginalised groups, in particular Black men. Their wordless choreography is amplified by the teacher's testimony, who sees the pandemic as a time during which histories of social injustice, anger, and grief collided: 'Are we mourning the little parts of our lives that we've lost', she asks the camera; 'we're feeling that sense of injustice, aren't we?'

In *Railway Worker*, directed by David Gilbert, a train dispatch operator named Kwame Bentil recalls how the pandemic affected his job, 'with not everyone treated equally'. Prior to the pandemic, he informs us, 'Anytime anybody needed help with anything, you'd be the first to walk over and give a hand.' 'But now that you can't be so close', he continues, 'everyone's got that you know real weird caution about them?' When one passenger makes a dramatic effort to avoid him, he suspects it's underpinned by racism rather

Figure 7 Jo Martin in *The Teacher* as part of Talawa Theatre's *Tales from the Front Line ... and other stories* (2020–1). (YouTube screengrab.)

Figure 8 Waddah Sinada (left) and Rhys Dennis (right) in *The Teacher* as part of
Talawa Theatre's *Tales from the Front Line . . . and other stories* (2020–1).
(YouTube screengrab.)

than health cautiousness. When white men board the train 'stinking of weed',
everyone presumes the smell is coming from him. Racism isn't confined to
white passengers, but it also spreads like a virus – a Black passenger he catches
smoking tells him that he will only stop for a white manager. In the course of
sharing his experience of the pandemic, the worker reveals that his real passion
is experimental Black music.

In *Primary School Teacher*, directed by Buffong, a woman (Yami
Löfvenberg) recalls the pain of denying pupils hugs during the pandemic.
When a child falls over, she tells us, 'they *need* someone to give them a little
cuddle'. She misses contact herself in other ways, with the loss of her
boxercise and salsa classes, which were all premised on close contact and
physical touch: 'Where before, salsa was all about the touch, you've got to
hold the person's hand, they move you, it's all to do with body contact.' The
same impulse follows through to the film *BREATHE*, directed by Ifrah Ismail.
Centring on an extended multimedia gallery dance performance by Chisara
Agor, a voice-over urges us to breathe, underneath a series of visual projec-
tions. 'You have the right to breathe a full-bodied breath', a voice-over assures
us, 'a right to heal'.

The UK Office for National Statistics reported that in 2019, 33 per cent of
the total workforce were in key worker occupations and industries, with the
largest group employed in health and social care (31 per cent), with 15 per cent
of key workers at moderate risk from the coronavirus (Office for National
Statistics 2020). While key workers were routinely celebrated in the media
and in public via the 'clap for carers' campaign, they were also likely to endure

Figure 9 Detail from the National Covid Memorial Wall, London, in appreciation of key workers (2021). Photograph by Ethan Doyle White. Courtesy of Wikipedia Commons.

more Covid-19 infections,[12] as well as mental distress.[13] A cynical interpretation of the clap for carers campaign is that it shone a light on those who were applauding in public more than it did on those who were working in frontline jobs, who needed adequate resources and remuneration rather than cheers. Talawa Theatre's project strives to rescue these workers from the reductive fate of news headlines or the compulsory performance of appreciation, and to flesh out their complex personal and professional lives. These frontline workers don't want to be applauded without protection or reward, but they appeal for the preservation of healthcare, education, and the arts for those enduring and surviving the losses of the pandemic (Figure 9).

Taryn Simon's *An Occupation of Loss* was co-commissioned by Artangel and Park Avenue Armory, first presented in New York in 2016 and London in 2018. In the London iteration, which took place inside a cavernous concrete building off Islington Green, attendees were invited to wander down three floors towards a pit deep underground. The surrounding walls were punctuated by window-shaped openings, like an unfinished façade in a subterranean amphitheatre, around which spectators could walk. Spikes of light cut through the space's vertical lines. In this inner circle of darkness, professional mourners from different cultures, mostly dressed in black, enacted sonic rituals of grief – singing, keening, playing music.

---

[12] See *The Lancet* Editorial, 'The plight of essential workers during the COVID-19 pandemic' (2020).

[13] See Greenberg, N., M. Docherty and S. Gnanapragasam and S. Wessely (2020), 'Managing mental health challenges faced by healthcare workers during Covid-19 pandemic'.

Scattered around the space, Armenian Yazidis recited a melodic mourning speech known as kilamê ser, a Cambodian ensemble presented Kantaoming funeral music, a Chinese Han participant wailed into a microphone while prostrating himself, and Greek performers delivered polyphonic panegyri. Within this sound-wall of grief, or at least of performed grief, we caught a sense of the world's grief, but also of art's capacity to hold it, discipline it, share it; to shift it from unformed feeling into an austere shape capable of containing it.

In 2020, Simon extended her original project in response to the pandemic, which not only unleashed death worldwide but rendered many of the professional mourners in her original project unable to work. In *An Occupation of Loss: Laments from Quarantine*, Simon created short films of some professional mourners in lockdown, grieving for those whose funerals they can't attend and for their lost lives and livelihoods. Sitting around a kitchen table in Athens, Nikos Menoudakis and Vangelis Kotsos sing a haunting panegyric using only their voices (Figure 10). The quarantine is like 'a divine act', they write in the accompanying statement, 'where we are all turned into monks that must 'face themselves, their lives, their truth'. Performing solo accordion, while singing a traditional lament, Aníbal González from Ecuador emphasises the loss of work as well as life: 'We have been affected in all areas – economy, society, and, in my case, in music. We have no work. Our artistic activities have been zeroed.' A Wayuu mourner from Venezuela, Ana Luisa Montiel Fernández, her head and torso covered with a striped hood, releases a lament that is both melodic and atonal, wavering between practised mourning and

Figure 10 Nikos Menoudakis (left) and Vangelis Kotsos (right) in *An Occupation of Loss: Laments from Quarantine* (2020). (Film screengrab.)

wild grief. 'In Guajira we are so afraid to get the virus', she says; 'The Wayuu people are against the cremation order imposed by the government. Cremating a body is against our culture and prevents the soul's journey through the Milky Way to Jepira. The soul is lost.'

Laments from Quarantine, in many ways, repeats the ideas and practices of the live installation. However, the fresh context and formal presentation of the material afford it new meaning and power. The performers are no longer mourning for an abstract, unknown figure, but grieving for their immediately affected families and communities, as well as the loss to their own livelihoods. 'Now death comes in a flash', Zamfira Mursean from Romania remarks, 'People do not have time to take care of the soul.'

Interviewed about the original iteration in *The New Yorker*, Simon observes that governments have not always treated professional mourners well because they disrupt the order of the state. While most government systems 'quantify death, reducing it to a list or a toll', Simon says it's 'unable to truly illuminate it', or allay the 'chaos and vulnerability of grief' (Simon in Mathew: 2020). For Simon, professional mourners have the capacity not just to mimic grief but to support it through ritualised sonic performance. In the context of the pandemic, Simon's claims about the inadequacy of governments' responses are all the more powerful, where the formal recitation of death tolls drowned out the sound of public grief as part of a strategic effort to render loss a bureaucratic exercise in accounting rather than a global traumatic event. Simon's digital iteration of *Laments from Quarantine* both mourns the loss of communal grief in public space as well as the loss of life and livelihoods in the face of pervasive obscuration.

Comforting Communities

While grief surfaces as an emotional as well as a physical response to loss, it also requires us to fashion new ways to maintain connections with the dead so that they can continue speaking to us. Our need to still hear the stories of the deceased underpinned Tara Theatre's audio-walk *Farewell*. Written by Sudha Bhuchar and directed by Abdul Shayek, the piece follows five characters and one Pug who died during the pandemic, which were informed by the testimonies of individuals with whom Bhuchar spoke. Tara Theatre is based in South West London, and its programme is led by exploring the South Asian perspectives of its community and championing South Asian artists.

In its original iteration, the audio-walk led listeners around Wandsworth, with stops in King George's Park, Garratt Lane Burial Ground, and a local park bench. Along the way, its subjects speak from beyond the grave, reflecting on their lives and deaths, crucially striving to offer comfort to those of us left behind. An Iranian photographer, Shahin, recalls his life as a closeted gay man and how he kept parts of this hidden while alive. As he describes his death, against a subtle track of thumping heartbeats and distant sirens, Shahin takes comfort in the fact that his last rites were performed by a priest, 'witnessed by a congregation of my dearest eight male gay friends', while his family in Iran mourned him over Zoom. While the hospital in which Shahin died is described as a 'warzone', he speaks directly to his mother to assure her: 'your son's cup was so full to the brim, I was drinking the aliveness, the nowness of life'.

Baby Han died in his mother's womb during the pandemic, and he speaks beyond death to paint a picture of what it was like for women to give birth at the time and the chaotic and sometimes lonely environment of hospitals. He tells us how his mother 'loves talking about me, not what I might have been, just that I was'. Ann, dying much older at 84, similarly enjoys people 'getting stuck in with all their anecdotes', recalling how she was the last to leave her neighbour-hood street parties, how she could 'drink them all under the table'. Ann remembers her niece taking her to the theatre, carried on a cloud of Chanel No. 5 and whiskey, and she imagines herself continuing to linger in that space. Jassie celebrated life and savoured her Punjabi culture and appreciates being cared for in her final days and remembered since her death. It's her husband, left behind, who concerns her now, and her story ends with her hoping that he might be able to speak about his grief with someone.

Covid-19 caused the biggest fall in life expectancy in England since the Second World War. Compared with 2019, life expectancy in 2020 fell by 1.3 years for males (from 80 years to 78.7) and 1 year for females (from 83.6 to 82.6) (Raleigh 2022). Deaths involving Covid-19 were highest for those aged 85 years and over (251 deaths), and this has been consistent throughout the coronavirus pandemic and reflects the highest overall hospital admission rates in the oldest age groups (Office for National Statistics 2023). Evidenced at the UK Covid-19 Inquiry on 31 October 2023, former chief scientist Patrick Vallance's pandemic diaries in August 2020 recorded that the government disregarded the elderly, with then Prime Minister Boris Johnson suggesting that his party considered Covid-19 as 'Nature's way of dealing with old people', and that they should accept their fates by allowing young people to 'get on with life' in order to keep the economy going (Weaver 2023). In the UK, the Office for National Statistics (2020a) reported that the risk of death involving the coronavirus was significantly higher among some ethnic groups. In particular, males in the Bangladeshi and Pakistani ethnic group were 1.8 times more likely to have a Covid-19-related death than White males; for females, the figure was 1.6 times more likely, with socio-economic disadvantage playing a leading disadvantaging factor.

Jacqueline Rose suggests that the pandemic calls on us to consider what counts as a dignified life and death, and how these conditions and questions are implicated in the fair distribution of resources. 'Can we imagine a world in which the deepest respect for death would exist alongside a fairer distribution of the wealth of the earth so that each individual has their share?', Rose asks; 'How can we ensure that death, as much as life, is given its dignity?' (2023: 15). A similar ethos undergirds Tara Theatre's project, insofar as it strives to dignify the lives and deaths of underrepresented voices by performing them into memory, which is to say, historical knowledge. As Annie Ernaux puts it in *The Years*, 'memory never stops. It pairs the dead with the living, real with imaginary beings, dreams with history' (2018 [2008]: 14). The figures in Tara Theatre's project have been marginalised in life, and their deaths may have taken place without fanfare, but the company insists we listen intently to their stories via site-specific audio-walks.

While Tara Theatre's project focuses on pandemic loss, its emphasis is on those who have died rather than those who are left behind. Each narrative functions as a consoling message to those who survive, assuring us that they have gleaned the most from life. In this, of course, it could be seen to sentimentally brush past the pain of loss, but it is forgiven for the ambition of striving to comfort those who continue to live. This emphasis also responds to a pattern observed within contemporary bereavement treatment. For example, research confirms that while for a long time healthy bereavement was considered a process of detachment from one's bonds, from the 1990s it emphasised the importance of continuing bonds through 'ongoing engagement with the deceased's memories and images, and internalization of their reconstructed image to enable positive psychological attachment' (Callaghan et al., 2013: 102–3). The voices of the dead in Tara Theatre's production, fulfilled and at peace, downplay the pain and injustice of their loss in the service of supporting their surviving community to develop bonds that sustain them in living.

Although the production premiered in South London, it has also toured the UK, mapping its community's losses across other communities and finding solace in their environments. The audio-walk allows us to explore local neighbourhoods more deeply, enhanced by overlain fictionalised accounts, while sidestepping some of the health risks associated with gathering indoors for theatre. Its public enactment implicitly counters the assumption that the outside world has become a dangerous, toxic space from which we should retreat. In listening to the stories via headphones, in the context of a nature walk, we are also invited to be consoled by the persistence of nature and all that has thrived in the face of loss. As an audio-based performance for one, *Final Farewell* is both intimate and lonesome, as we listen to stories of the dead on our own, without synchronised participation. As the voices speak in isolation, so too must we listen on our own. But *Final Farewell* is also a walk that compels its participants to perform a scattered procession for the dead within the neighbourhoods of its production, affording those who died alone or were buried quickly without friends and family the final farewell they missed.

Voice to Outrage

Jo Clifford and Lesley Orr's memorial service, *The Covid Requiem*, also used ritual and music to mourn and commemorate the dead (Figure 11). The project arose out of a sense that people needed communal experiences to remember the dead in response to the lack of public memorial services and the absence of a national strategy. Clifford, a playwright and former nurse, and Orr, a theologian and historian, developed a script to 'to celebrate the stories and lives of those lost in the pandemic' (Clifford in Brown 2021).

Presented as a ritual, reflections on loss, death, and grief are organised around recalling specific individuals while delivering prompts for us to pause and remember. In the outdoor iteration at the Pitlochry Festival Theatre in 2021, accompanied by Duncan Chisholm's traditional musical composition, attendees were invited to walk through the woods, offering the natural world

Figure 11 Jo Clifford (left) and Lesley Orr in *The Covid Requiem* (2021). Photograph by Rhys Watson. Courtesy of Jo Clifford and Lesley Orr.

as an antidote to experiences of death, and the privatising experiences of compulsory isolation and 'stay at home' orders. Directed by Amy Liptrott, those in the audience-congregation were urged to bring a stone to the ceremony. At the end of the ceremony, they were invited to use the stone to build a memorial cairn, which originally covered Neolithic graves, locating our need to mark our grief as part of an ancient, cross-generational communal impulse. The word 'grief' has roots in the proto-Indo-European root *gwerə-*, meaning 'heavy'. Here, the gesture of putting down stones also symbolises a putting down of one's emotional burdens in the service of a collective endeavour. To grieve, in Clifford and Orr's intervention, means to share its weight socially and culturally via its narration, ritual enactment, and material demarcation.

According to Orr, 'many had to die alone', and many were 'consigned to the grave without their stories being told' (Clifford and Orr 2021). Unable to visit one another, to bear witness to grief, according to Clifford, 'we have still to complete the business of grieving [. . .] To tell the stories that could not be told. To bear witness to the grief that could not be spoken. To find the words that could not be said' (Clifford and Orr 2021).

Interlacing their voices, the pair warmly expresses their wish to:

Orr	To speak out our anger.
	To give voice to our outrage.
Clifford	To find a way to forgive.
Orr	To give thanks for those who looked after our loved ones
	Be thankful for those who looked after the sick,
	Always at risk to themselves.
Clifford	And so to find hope in their compassion and humanity.
Orr	To dream that change is possible in this world.
Clifford	To name the names. (Clifford and Orr 2021)

While naming specific individuals and embellishing details as supplied by attendees (Charles, who loved to explore the hills; Gordon, the car buff who loved his classic Citroen cars), the refrain spoken by both repeats:

> We miss you.
> It's so hard to manage now you're gone.
> You gave us so much.
> And what you gave us will always be with us.
> Thank you. We love you. (Clifford and Orr 2021)

Although mired in grief, the ceremony also imagines a time when, as Orr puts it, we might be able to 'recall and remember without the painful tug of grief/And our sadness will be like something washed down by the river to the sea' (Clifford and Orr 2021).

While the text has largely remained the same since the original iteration, the production's site and musical accompaniment have adapted to new locations. A scaled-up iteration in 2022 was more firmly rooted in a religious context by taking place at St Mary's Cathedral, Edinburgh. Here, Clifford and Orr were accompanied by the thirty-strong cathedral choir singing Gabriel Fauré's *Requiem to* remember those who died and those who continue to grieve. According to Clifford, the ceremony is a reminder that 'we may need to pass through the winter of grief; but that it will be followed by the new hope of spring' (2021).

In Marina Carr's *Woman and Scarecrow*, a woman struggles to die as she surveys her life and tries to balance her crimes. 'Grief can be measured! Grief can be calibrated!' she wryly insists, 'Ten pints of grief I can swallow but not a drop more!' (2006: 38). But in *The Covid Requiem*, grief resists being reduced to data or contained by quantitative maps – it's beyond measure and calibration. In delivering their anecdotes, commentary, and remembrances, Clifford and Orr perform roles most commonly associated with religious celebrants. But their formation also calls to mind the regular news reports during the height of the pandemic delivered by politicians and medics recounting new spikes and dips in death tolls. This mode of delivery was all too mechanical while obscuring the impact on individual lives and experiences of loss. In their warmth and attentiveness to individual lives, the service humanises a political climate intent on downplaying the pandemic's effects, with Clifford and Orr reminding us that we must immerse ourselves in the dark sounds of winter before we can appreciate the bright stirrings of spring.

Climates of Grief

A recurring feature of the works explored in this section is the siting of performance and ritual encounters outdoors, drawing audiences into the natural world and public spaces deemed hazardous by Covid-19 regulations. In this, they appeal to us to rethink the public sphere and natural world during a time of disease, but also to reckon with environmental loss and preservation on a larger scale. The pandemic took place at a time when many people were also grappling with environmental grief, as a response to the steady and likely irreparable destruction of the planet. As Kriss Kevorkian defines it, 'Environmental grief is the grief reaction stemming from the environmental loss of ecosystems caused by either natural or human-made events' (2020: 217).

While, in one very real sense, the pandemic and environmental loss are distinct phenomena operating in different temporalities, in another, they are intricately intertwined. In the European Commission Science for Environment Policy report, 'Future Brief: Covid-19 and the Environment: Links, Impacts and Lessons Learned', its authors report that '[t]he increasing frequency of epidemics and pandemics since 2000 has been linked to global change factors such as land use change causing encroachment onto wild areas, global wildlife trade, live wildlife markets, intensive agricultural practices, climate change, global tourism and poor air quality' (2022: 12), and practices 'which increase human–wildlife contact' (2022: 12). Climate change is likely to cause future risk of pandemics, the report adds, by 'movement of pathogens – alongside people, wildlife, reservoirs and vectors – in ways that lead to new species contacts, increased contacts and disruption of natural host-pathogen dynamics' (2022: 26).

In the outdoor performances discussed here, we are invited to repopulate public space and to seek solace and comfort in the natural world. However, the additional context of environmental loss due to climate change subtly calls on us to value the natural world with renewed commitment. Human death and environmental loss are not coincidental here, but rather the context of the former is subtly given to spur a response to the latter.

Writing about Black poetic form, and in particular the work of Audre Lorde, Kevin Quashie describes aliveness as 'contagious being through openness, this tingling consciousness or habitat of sense that is being in the world' (2021: 21). For Quashie, aliveness describes a relation 'where the focus is on one's preparedness for encounter rather than the encounter itself' (2021: 21). While the works explored in this section respond to grief by naming the dead and giving form to subjectivity, they also tingle with the kind of aliveness elaborated by Quashie, which is a readiness for being in the world again.

There are days when it feels like the pandemic happened decades ago, days when it feels like it was last month, and days when reports of surges suggest that we are still living through it. Indeed, while the World Health Organisation announced on 5 May 2023 that Covid-19 was no longer a public emergency, more than three years after it began, its dangers and after-effects persist, though the impact of grief remains poorly addressed. The time of traumatic events, as psychoanalysis teaches us, is bundled and hazy (Caruth 1995). Our minds protect us by containing and displacing pain to make life in the present bearable, but without dutifully recognising and living through the grief, it will only come back to disturb and derail us in other ways. As the work discussed here conveys, we owe it to the dead to mark their lives, so that they are not forgotten in the fog of time that would render their lives insignificant. But we also owe it to those who go on living to allow their losses to be grieved and commemorated, and to help brace ourselves to avoid and meet future loss. We need monuments to commemorate the dead – to fix people and events in history in durable stone and bronze. But we also require theatre and performance to feel the power of temporarily coming together as a collective, and to rehearse for the inevitability of departing on our own, as we all must eventually do.

4 Rupture and Rebirth: Reassembling Anew

While the pandemic was experienced by most of us as a time of compulsory lockdowns, a series of Black Lives Matter protests, triggered by the killing of George Floyd at the hands of the police in Minneapolis, Minnesota on 25 May 2020, saw public spaces around the world being flooded with people again. In the UK, these protests converged with the toppling of the statue of slave trader Edward Colston in Bristol on 7 June of the same year, his effigy theatrically dislodged and rolled into the River Avon by a group of young people (four of whom were charged with criminal damage and subsequently cleared), cheered on by a local crowd.

The origins of the Black Lives Matter protests that surrounded Floyd's death preceded the pandemic, spurred on by social unrest in response to the treatment of Black people at the hands of the police in the USA. The movement began in July 2013 on social media following the acquittal of George Zimmerman in the shooting death of African-American teen Trayvon Martin the previous year, gaining traction following the killing of Michael Brown and Eric Garner in 2014. The dying words of Garner and Floyd, 'I can't breathe', which supplied Black Lives Matter's slogan, synthesised the racial and health crises that defined the period, particularly for the Black and global majority communities who were disproportionately affected by Covid-19, owing to contributing vectors of socio-economic inequality. As Talawa Theatre's *Tales from the Front Line … and other stories* documented in the previous section, Black and global majority heritage staff made up a sizable proportion of frontline and key workers who put their own health at risk in the service of supporting and protecting others' lives.

While protest may be read as an act of aggression and even violence, it's frequently also a response to experiences of loss and injustice. Writing about the time of slavery and its persisting impact, Saidiya Hartman asks, 'How might we understand mourning, when the event has yet to end?' (2002: 758). Hartman is referring to the fact that the effects of slavery are still experienced around the world, as 'the diffuse violence and the everyday routines of domination, which continue to characterize black life but are obscured by their everydayness' (772). But as the Black Lives Matter protests recognise, it also continues in the structural subjugation by the state as well as via direct violence enacted on Black bodies.

In an article in *The New York Times Magazine*, Claudia Rankine recalls asking a friend what it's like being the mother of a Black son. 'The condition of black life is one of mourning', she replied, as at any moment she might lose her son (2015). Mourning, in Rankine's writing, is not just for what has happened but for what is anticipated; an unending grief for those who have died and for those who are most likely to die prematurely. Mourning in the context of ongoing violence, we may conclude, cannot be experienced without some form of reactive violence, as a response against those who refuse to allow grief to be expressed. In colonial histories, the time of violence and the time of grief are intricately intertwined.

Colston's statue was erected in 1895, not just to honour a philanthropist as his protectors have posited, but as a monument to the intensification of British colonial violence that was happening in Africa at the time. Since the 1990s, unsuccessful appeals had been aired for the statue to be removed by those who saw it as a glorification of racist history. These calls for action, as Dan Hicks has argued, were 'not about iconoclasm, but about ridding our cities of the enduring infrastructures of white supremacy, tracking and tracing a disease that attacks the ability to breathe' (Hicks 2020). In the toppling of Colston's statue in Bristol, we were not just witnessing a protest against the city's colonial history, but the ways in which that history and its legacy refused to let Black lives be adequately grieved, including during the pandemic. Here, as Hicks phrases it, 'the virus of white supremacy' and Covid-19 collided with and compounded one another, erupting in a gesture mirrored by similar efforts around the world to remove racist statues and monuments, which insisted that those Black and global majority communities most affected by both be allowed to breathe and to grieve.[14] The capacity to breathe and grieve, in this correlation, is given as a fundamental precondition to living. This intersection was captured by the numerous placards that surrounded the protest that eventually took Colston's statue down, including 'I Can't Breathe' and 'Racism is a Pandemic' (Figure 12). Protests are also performances – embodied, aestheticised and dramaturgically shaped – however impromptu. The Colston protest was not without its power struggles, however, as exemplified by accusations that Colston was felled by white locals. The sense that white people tried to control

---

[14] Following the mass shooting of Black people in a church in Charleston, South Carolina in 2015, more than 140 public confederate monuments have been removed in the USA with two-thirds taken down following the murder of George Floyd in 2020. See Berkowitz, B. and A. Blanco (2021), 'A record number of Confederate monuments fell in 2020, but hundreds still stand. Here's where'.

Figure 12 Placards surrounding the fallen statue of Edward Colson, Bristol, 2020. Photograph by Caitlin Hobbs. Courtesy of Wikipedia Commons.

the narrative was compounded when artist Mark Quinn installed a statue on Colson's vacated plinth overnight of the Black protester Jen Reid, *A Surge of Power* (2020), without consulting the city's residents. While the subject's hand is raised in a Black power salute, triumph was seen to be too premature a gesture, and not one to be called by a white male artist, when violence and grief abounded.

When Colson's statue was eventually salvaged and installed in Bristol's MShed Museum, on one level, it seemed to echo the opening lines of Chris Marker, Alain Resnais, and Ghislain Cloquet's film essay about African art in European museums, *Les Statues Meurent Aussi* (1953): 'When people die, they enter history. When statues die, they enter art.' But placed horizontally, like a graffitied corpse, efforts were at least taken to indicate that the statue now resided more ambiguously between history and art, its symbolism as a celebratory monument to imperial racism undercut. If Black Lives Matter protests saw people flood the public sphere in the name of racial justice, they also pre-empted a wider appetite to occupy public spaces after quarantine injunctions. In a discussion of how 'stay at home' orders led to spikes in domestic violence, Jacqueline Rose conjures an image of 'isolation with interiority, solitude leeched of its inner dimension, loneliness without redress' (2023: 70). Compulsory aloneness, in this formulation, was not always the life-saving strategy it was presented as but a form of emotional and psychic evisceration experienced most sharply by the most vulnerable and marginalised. While stay-at-home orders may have protected us from pathogens, they also enacted other forms of emotional and social violence; they were not sustainable in the long term.

As Rose's critique of compulsory isolation indicates, we can only be alone for so long; eventually, we have to find ways of being together again. Even as pandemic theatres supported grief, they also rehearsed new ways of uniting in shared time and space, urging us to step away from isolation and into whatever new forms of communal gathering might have become possible. In the case of theatre, this impulse was also reflected in the gradual improvement in audience attendance figures in 2022 compared to previous pandemic years (Hemley 2023).

Writing about the politics of assembly, in the wake of the Tahrir Square uprising in 2012, Judith Butler writes that 'debates about popular demonstrations tend to be governed either by fears of chaos or by radical hope for the future, though sometimes fear and hope get interlocked in complex ways' (2015: 1–2). The conditions Butler describes were thrown into sharp relief during the pandemic, as a result of bans on public assembly, curfews, and social distancing. While these were ostensibly designed to protect against the spread of Covid-19, they also impacted civil rights, in particular 'the freedoms of expression, assembly and association' (Buyse 2021). In some constituencies, these were seized upon by administrations intent on shrinking civic space and curtailing the right to protest and demonstrate. In the UK, the Public Order Act 2023 granted increased powers to the police in England and Wales to crack down on public disruption and protest, strengthening those previously enshrined in the Police, Crime, Sentencing and Courts Act 2022.

It's against this political backdrop that the politics of assembly, in the works considered in this section, must be seen. On a social level, assembly means the coming together online, or via physical proximity and contact in shared space, and in a political sense, it signals the potential for these modes and creative interventions to pressure political climates that willfully manufacture alienation as a form of social regulation. Theatrical assembly both sidesteps the restrictions of political assembly while also positing itself as a tool in the same pursuit. I argue that the experiments in assembly discussed here grieve and commemorate our losses, in fear and hope, but also orient us towards imagining and participating in new forms of cultural, social, and political assembly premised on recognising shared experiences of loss.

Here, I explore productions that emphasised new forms of assembly as central to the processing of pandemic grief by socialising it culturally and channelling it towards political resistance and transformation. It focuses on work that questions the relationship between digital and in-person assembly while also stressing the need for new forms of gathering to respond to issues of ecological, cultural, social, and political urgency. Among the works explored include Nina Segal's *Assembly* (2021), which queried how humans might come together to respond to the social and ecological fallout of the pandemic; Dante or Die's *Skin Hunger* (2020), which explored the need for human touch in the wake of the pandemic, in a manner that resonates with Fevered Sleep's grief works; the Belfast Ensemble's *Mass* (2021), which presented immersive opera as a form of secular group worship, including for the queer artists represented in it; and THISISPOPBABY's *Wake* (2022), which staged an exuberant wake.

Dispersed Citizenship

Nina Segal's *Assembly* explores the capacity of new forms of human assembly to rebuild the world. Directed by Joseph Hancock, in this surreal digital artwork, a citizens' assembly is asked by a facilitator to 'imagine a different version of the future'. On the brink of apocalypse, with the threat of 'rising water' and 'fireballs' posing an immediate danger, the group is tasked with confronting climate disaster, waste disposal, human inaction, community collapse, and the mundane distractions that can divert our attention from the bigger picture. Armed with gas masks, those assembled are given one day to devise a plan.

Originally created for the stage but adapted to be live-streamed on YouTube during the pandemic, the premise of Segal's play is an investigation into the power of human assembly in shared space, especially in theatre. The online version necessarily explored the capacity of digital formats to bring people together to tackle global issues, as well as the frustrations and limits of digital congregation. Here, action gets delayed by tea-drinking and eating, and the allure of petty personal wishes in the face of communal need.

Represented through a mix of graphics, animation, and cardboard costumes, the cast is live-streamed from sixteen locations, including the Donmar

Warehouse in Covent Garden, London; an industrial estate in Cardiff, Wales; and a bedroom in Westminster, London. Graphics and design from Andrzej Goulding and Raphael Pimlott create a sense of ludic disorder, while Max Pappenheim's melancholy score amplifies a dystopian soundscape.

Writing about the conjunction of the Black Lives Matter protests and the pandemic, Andrew Asibong claims that 'when we feel afraid of death, dying, or – perhaps even worse – the possibility that we may be dying inside, and when we don't feel we have sufficient containment from other human beings to help us make it through these fearful feelings, intensely emotional interactions with certain kinds of moving image may help us to stay connected to the endangered aliveness within our psyches' (Asibong 2022: 8). While Asibong writes as a psychotherapist, he makes the case for the possibility that a 'multiplicity of cultural methods' may ward off the experience or threat of psychic deadness.

Assembly is convincing in its vision that coming together, with a sense of collaborative commitment, is a precondition to solving global problems. But in its playful chaos, compounded by split-screen techniques, accidental freezes, and time delays, it is also keenly aware of the communicative and social challenges to ecological and political transformation. While the production ultimately feels less optimistic about digital assembly of any kind, including theatre, to tackle the issues it addresses, it makes a strong case for the necessity of playful experimentation with whatever tools are available to attempt the urgent work of resisting individual, collective, or ecological deadness or extinction.

Dying for Touch

One of the most striking images that circulated during the pandemic came from hospital wards in Brazil in 2020, in which two surgical gloves filled with warm water were used to hold the hands of a sick or dying patient when no one else could be present. The 'hand of god', as the object became known, represented nurses' efforts to allow patients to feel a sense of warm touch, in the face of understaffing and quarantine, often in the last moments of their lives (Figure 13). What patients needed most in these hours, the nurses knew, as many theatre makers have long believed of audiences, was to make close contact with others.

Digital and distanced communication is always haunted by the lack of touch – we touch with our eyes and ears, certainly, but the quality of touch is different from touching skin or proximate body contact. In Section 1, we get a sense of this distinction in those productions that are concerned with bodily absence in the theatre, particularly with the absence of the audience in shared time and space.

Dante or Die explored our grief and longing for human touch in *Skin Hunger*. This one-to-one performance, set in a hidden chapel in London's West End, was

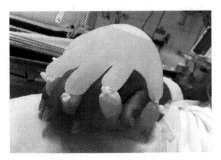

Figure 13 'The Hand of God' (2020), constructed by nurses in Brazil to comfort Covid-19 patients. Taken from Twitter where it circulated widely.

originally organised around a dramaturgy of haptic denial and longing. Spectators rotated around a station of three performers, separated by a large plastic sheet, forming a quarantine chamber that divided the space. These sheets resemble those used to quarantine patients in hospital settings and call to mind the face masks used on a daily basis to limit the spread of disease, and marked everyone, 'regardless of one's subjective ethical intention', as Benjamin Bratton puts it, 'a contagion vector just the same' (2022: 103). Videos playing on screens reflected on the impact of the loss of touch during the pandemic, echoing a body of research that confirmed that touch deprivation during Covid-19 was 'associated with higher anxiety and greater loneliness' (von Mohr et al. 2021: 1). Directed by Daphna Attias, the piece was composed of three monologues, delivered as if speeches to ex-lovers, including Ann Akinjirin's *Our Hands*, Tim Crouch's *The Sessions*, and Sonia Hughes's *Touch the Flesh*, with each contribution exploring the role of touch in our lives and the effects of its loss.

In Akinjirin's contribution, a performer (Rachel-Leah Hosker) describes feeling self-conscious about her hands: how she never liked them, never thought they were soft enough. She casts us in the role of her former partner, reaching against the plastic divider to ask, 'Who's going to hold my hand now? Will anyone ever hold my hand again?' (Akinjirin 2021: 39) (Figure 14). In Crouch's text, a troubled man (Terry O'Donovan) reckons with his responsibility for the breakdown of a relationship. To the audience member observing him, he appeals: 'Hold me and tell me it's okay, to hold me and say it's okay' (Crouch 2021: 53). The phrase 'touch the flesh' anchors Hughes's piece, which focuses on a father's memory loss due to dementia. Performer Oseloka Obi plays a son who recites his father's stories for him, his body bridging the widening gap in his father's cognitive function.

While the plastic sheet dividing the performance space creates a quarantine chamber, it also evokes all those objects we used to separate and protect

Figure 14 Rachel-Leah Hosker performs in *Skin Hunger on Film* (2021).
(Film screengrab.)

ourselves during the pandemic: masks, plastic gloves, doors, and digital screens. It additionally invites us to weigh up what was lost and gained in this endeavour. These material conditions may have limited infectious illness, but they affected our emotional and mental lives in negative ways. This production is an appeal to the power of touch in our everyday lives, but also to the importance of physical proximity to theatre, which digital practices cannot precisely replicate.

Freya Verlander, writing about the performance, argues that 'the desire for touch' (2022: 8) endured during the pandemic, a time defined by Richard Kearney for its 'eclipse of the tactile' (2021: 3). For Kearney, 'COVID-19 signaled the compromise of our "animal" senses – touch, taste, and smell – compelling us to live through the eye more than at any time in history' (2021: 135). A hunger for lost touch is given dramaturgical shape in this production, Verlander argues, as an '*almost* touch that plays at the interstices between contagion and containment, between performance and public health' (15), which anticipates a future 'when skin-to-skin contact [. . .] will return' (14). Also produced as a film (*Skin Hunger on Film*, 2021), *Skin Hunger* doesn't commit to the idea that skin-to-skin contact is possible only in live performance, but accedes to the capacity of what Kearney refers to as 'telehaptic modes of communication', which combine 'virtual and tactile bodies', in challenging dualistic divisions between the mind and the body, biological life and digital technology (Kearney 2021: 139).

Reflecting on his own mourning at the death of his mother, Roland Barthes wrote, 'Each of us has his own rhythm of suffering' (Barthes 2009 [2012]: 162).

In Barthes's account, feeling and movement are intertwined – grief can be dynamic and immobile, yielding and resistant. We catch a glimpse of this in Fevered Sleep's short dance film *8 Tender Solitudes*, which also explored the impact of the loss of touch during the pandemic, through movement and music. Working with seven dancers, who perform to a score by Kate Whitley, the piece captured a sense of the loneliness and yearning that characterised isolation during the pandemic. Here, each dancer performs alone, their bodies often pressed up-close to the camera, as if they are trying to surpass it and reach the viewer. Following Kearney, we might think of this too as a telehaptic mode of contact, though the dancers straining to reach through the lens appear less satisfied with this screen barrier.

While *8 Tender Solitudes* was created in response to the pandemic, it builds on Fevered Sleep's earlier project, *This Grief Thing*. Structured around so-called 'grief gatherings', textiles, and a billboard campaign, the project was developed as a non-theatrical mode intended to encourage conversation around grief. Having hosted numerous workshops on the subject, the company opened clothes shops around the UK and online, stocked with clothes featuring phrases collected from these encounters, including 'Grief Is Like The Weather', 'Grief = Love', and 'Don't Panic If I Cry' so that they could make their way into the world to raise awareness of the subject. In 2020, during the pandemic, the project migrated online and took the form of speakers coming together in conversation.

Fevered Sleep's approach suggests that grief resists theatricalisation, or at least that theatricalisation comes with the risk of suppressing other forms of necessary experiencing and expression. Grief, here, is a *thing* – a difficult object that must be circled and navigated; spoken about and touched, rather than performed. As with Dante or Die's *Skin Hunger*, for Fevered Sleep, grief is felt most profoundly as an absence of contact and touch, and their work prioritises creating spaces to sustain forms of proximity and intimacy.

Where Death Dies a Little

The Belfast Ensemble tore through the divisions of plastic and screen with their production, *MASS*. A collaboration between the company, OUTBURST Queer Arts Festival, and the Ulster Orchestra, *MASS* was an ambitious, large-scale event that took over the Belfast Telegraph Printworks, one of the city's most iconic empty spaces. This immersive, multidisciplinary event was part oratorio, part rave, featuring classical singers Giselle Allen, Sarah Richmond, Christopher Cull, and John Porter, and commissioned visual artworks by queer film-makers from across the world, including Madonna Adib, Mariah

Garnett, Simone Harris, Mohammad Shawky Hassan, Vi Grunvald, Paulo Mendel, and Debalina Majumder.

The Belfast Ensemble focuses on music-based performance and queer aesthetics and politics. *Abomination: A DUP Opera* (2019) was concerned with the after-effects of Iris Robinson, a one-time DUP MP, claiming on BBC Radio Ulster's *Stephen Nolan Show* in 2008 that homosexuality was an 'abomination' that made her feel 'sick'. During the pandemic in 2020, the company produced a digital performance of Mark Ravenhill's *Ten Plagues* (2011), which reflected on plagues throughout history, from the Great Plague of London to AIDS. In Ravenhill's script, the speaker grieves:

> Too many gone
> To mourn another
> We all are plagued
> Our hearts are gone
> Our bodies live
> We walking dead
> About the city now (Ravenhill 2011: 20–1)

In my last book, I wrote about how the digital version of *Ten Plagues* formed part of a cluster of queer performances produced during the pandemic to comment on Covid-19 through the prism of AIDS (Walsh 2023). In a similar way, *MASS* finds inspiration for post-pandemic life among the queer cultural production that survived AIDS, but in a way that prioritises the boisterous collision of bodies, cultures, and art rather than their careful containment, as in *Ten Plagues*.

The word 'mass', in this production, resonates with multiple meanings. In one very particular sense, it denotes a Catholic congregation and religious service, which in Northern Ireland evokes the region's historically most discriminated against community. In a more general sense, as in *Assembly*, it conjures a large gathering of people and artworks. *MASS* appeals to some of the values that underpin religious ceremonies but rejects its objects and institutions of devotion. Instead, it celebrates the sacred in the profane; the joyful and queer coming together of bodies, communities, and art to herald a break in pandemic restrictions and to summon enthusiasm for post-pandemic life. The empty Printworks space is both a material example and a metaphor for the isolation and abandonment that characterised the pandemic, utterly transformed in this gesture of cathartic theatrical excess. According to the company's promotional material, *MASS* represented an 'evolution in the way we experience live music and queer ritual, dancing in the spirit of celebration and power in the collective'.

During the Covid-19 pandemic, reports of sexual orientation and transgender hate crimes recorded by UK police forces rose, reflecting how a fear of death or a denial of grief, which are one and the same, can also be met with projected violence. As reported in *The Guardian*, from January to August 2021, at least 14,670 homophobic hate crime offences were recorded, compared with 11,841 during the same interval in 2020 and 10,817 in 2019. Police recorded 2,129 transphobic offences between January and August 2021, far exceeding the 1,606 offences in 2020 and 1,602 in 2019. Responding to these figures, Leni Morris, chief executive of the LGBT anti-violence charity Galop, suggested that queer people were being blamed for the pandemic 'because perpetrators thought the pandemic was an act of God – because of the existence of LGBT+ people – or because of the community's association with the last major pandemic in people's minds, and that's the HIV Aids pandemic' (Chao-Fong 2021). Attacks on queer people were also accompanied by violence against Asian and Pacific Island people, who were also perceived as agents of the disease.[15] Understood in this context, the Belfast Ensemble's *MASS* signals a commitment to celebrating communion, and in particular queer congregation, as a response to the violence projected onto marginalised communities.

A similar approach guided Dublin-based THISISPOPBABY's *WAKE*. This cabaret-style production drew on the Irish tradition of a wake for the dead to mourn loss by celebrating life. Directed by Jennifer Jennings and Phillip McMahon, with text by Carys D. Coburn, *WAKE* was originally conceived as a 'frenzy of ritual, rave, grief and joy' intended to celebrate 'community, regeneration, and the magic of collective catharsis'. Described by the Dublin-based company as 'an adrenaline shot for the city', *WAKE* acknowledged the losses of the pandemic by rousing us back to life in a celebration of communal gathering.

THISISPOPBABY's production is structured as a performance cabaret, with elements of theatre, spoken word, music, circus, and dance woven into a glossy spectacle. Gymnasts, pole dancers, a DJ, and spoken word performance jostle alongside more traditional forms such as Irish dance, accordion music, and rousing writing. In this collision of forms, *WAKE* communicates a sense of how traditional and contemporary forms speak to each other across time and how all of them need to be harnessed to help support audiences and communities to move beyond the destruction and stasis that defined the pandemic period.

According to Christina Sharpe, 'Wakes are processes; through them we think about the dead and about our relation to them; they are rituals through which to enact grief and memory. Wakes allow those among the living to mourn the

---

[15] For more on these statistics, see Movement Advancement Project (2020).

passing of the dead through ritual' (2016: 21). In the Irish wake tradition, mourners gather in the homes of the dead to keep vigil over the corpse before it's buried. Since the 1800s, Irish emigrants moving to the USA were given an American wake to mark their departure to a country from which they were unlikely to ever return. But an Irish wake is not an entirely sombre experience – it's also a celebration, characterised by the community bringing food and drink for all to consume, and storytelling and music-playing. This is how the lives of the deceased are marked, and those of the living are comforted. Indeed, recent research has suggested that compared to the UK, the social, communal nature of Irish wakes may positively support the bereaved in coming to terms with loss (Hyland et al., 2023: 9). For audiences to participate in the theatrical production *WAKE*, understood in this context, requires us to watch over the dead and celebrate their lives, including how they continue to enrich us.

THISISPOPBABY's production does not shy away from the death that motors its engine. 'This is the wake for everything that's never coming back', emcee Felicia Olusanya tells us, 'This is the christening of the gorgeous radical nothing we're facing' (Figure 15). 'Feel free to feel sad', she assures us, 'provided you're also open to feeling something else'. Here, rebirth is a form of rupture, mourning a form of rapture, and life and death are given to be always intertwined. *WAKE*'s response to grief is not to leave the dead behind but to take

Figure 15 Felicia Olusanya performs in front of the cast of THISISPOPBABY's *WAKE* (2022). Photograph by Ruth Medjber. Courtesy of THISISPOPBABY.

them with us. We must die a little ourselves, the emcee advises, to make space
for the dead within ourselves. In this process of death producing life, the wake is
a ritual 'where death dies itself a little'. This dying of death becomes a clarion
call for an excess of life, which we live not only for ourselves but for those lives
we carry inside us:

> Living with the dead means more partying, more drinking, more fucking,
> more cooking elaborate meals, more glitter, more blood, more champagne,
> more cum, MORE ALL OF THE GOOD STUFF not less, precisely because
> the dead can't join in, so we have to do it, all of it, on their behalf.

Philosopher Vinciane Despret has suggested that the notion that the dead
have 'no destiny other than nonexistence' (2021 [2015]: 4) is a local and
historically recent idea, dating back to the nineteenth century. Associating the
dead with the non-existent, Despret tells us, was a way to break the authority of
religious institutions over the bereaved, producing the prescription: 'We *have to*
do the *work* of mourning' (5), that is, to perceive the dead as firmly beyond life,
beyond reach. The idea that mourning is a task to be completed was advanced by
Freud, after which, he states, 'our libido is once more free (in so far as we are
still young and active) to replace the lost objects by fresh ones equally or more
precious' (2001 [1916]: 307). But in Despret's work, grief may not necessarily
mean detaching from those we've lost as part of a staged process of mourning,
but involve maintaining creative connections with them.

Drawing on biographical sources and local customs, Despret counters this
dominant western way of thinking by describing how the dead continue to
intervene in and interfere with life, beyond being mere phantasms or hallucin-
ations, with 'ways of being' (8) that call upon us to maintain their existence. In
Despret's work, the dead don't necessarily ask us to mourn them into nonexistence, but ask to be inscribed in space (10), and they need 'care, attention,
activities, a milieu that, if not conducive or welcoming, is at least not too hostile'
(9). 'The requirement to give them "more" life', Despret insists, 'falls on us' (6).

WAKE conveys a similar sense that grief requires us not to leave the dead
behind, but to continue listening to their voices and give them 'more life'. As in
Despret's work, the production functions as a vehicle for 'those who remain',
who commit to maintaining relationships with the dead. These individuals, as
Despret writes, 'explore the successful setting up of relationships with care,
attention, wisdom and much interest. They create new ways of using places and
have a go at composing the milieus [...] they make an effort to rise to the
difficulty of the challenge of losing someone – and learning to find him or her
again' (12). This sentiment also echoes through Derek Jarman's film *Blue*
(1993), which was made as he was dying of AIDS, with Jarman's voice intoning

over a washed-out screen: 'I hear the voices of dead friends/Love is life that lasts forever'. Love, in and through art, is how life endures, even in the face of shattering loss.

The question of how best to remember the dead has a particular resonance within queer culture. Writing about the impact of AIDS on himself and the queer community that surrounded him, David Wojnarowic insisted on making grief public; on turning mourning into a demonstration that made its effects visible to those whose negligence contributed to unnecessary death, in particular politicians:

> IT'S HEALTHY TO MAKE THE PRIVATE PUBLIC, BUT THE WALLS OF THE ROOM OR CHAPEL ARE THIN AND UNNECESSARY. ONE SIMPLE STEP CAN BRING IT OUT INTO A MORE PUBLIC SPACE. DON'T GIVE ME A MEMORIAL IF I DIE. GIVE ME A DEMONSTRATION. (1999: 206)

MASS and *WAKE* follow in this tradition by creating spaces for grief outside of churches and funeral homes, allowing them to become occasions of demonstration as well as celebration in the face of loss.

For Antonin Artaud, a new understanding of theatre's potential comes into being with the plague. In this 'true theater', as Artaud describes it, 'a play disturbs the senses' repose, frees the repressed unconscious, incites a kind of virtual revolt (which moreover can have its full effect only if it remains virtual), and imposes on the assembled collectivity an attitude that is both difficult and heroic' (1958 [1938]: 28). Something of this difficult and heroic revolt ripples through the works explored in this section, which oppose the fear of collective assembly informed by efforts to contain disease, by celebrating the necessity of emotional, social, and cultural exchange to the sustenance of life once biomedical danger has waned.

Anyone who created theatre during the pandemic or made plans to attend it will know that assembly was never guaranteed but always at risk of being derailed by illness or lockdowns. Throughout this Element, pandemic theatre has been caught up in a tension to simultaneously acknowledge and stage loss and to find new ways of coming together again. This impulse peaks in this section, with productions that insist on the necessity of our stepping out of isolation to collectivise, online or in-person, in order to socialise grief and channel it for cultural and political change.

Theatre has long been imagined as a haunted form, shadowed by the ghosts of the past who occupy its spaces (Carlson 2001). But for the works explored here, the dead don't linger gloomily over our shoulders, but supply the life force that propels us forward in cultural production, social participation, and striving for political transformation. For THISISPOPBABY, the function of the Irish wake is to live life to the full on behalf of those who cannot experience it for themselves. In this, we see how theatre might not only be understood as a melancholic space in which the dead inevitably tug our attention backwards, but as a jubilant, riotous machine that insists we take them with us.

Coda: Life Worth Living

When Elizabeth Bishop opens her poem 'One Art' (1976) claiming that '[t]he art of losing isn't hard to master', she captures just how ordinary and pervasive loss is: the fate of so many objects, places, and people. Everything, eventually, passes hands or dies. Her verse skips confidently through a litany of losses, attempting to assure us, not without knowing overstatement, that at least she has mastered hers. Bishop enacts it too, in the tight holding structure of the villanelle, which refuses to let grief leak between its lines. In the closing parenthetical demand – '(*Write* it!)' – Bishop urges herself, and perhaps her readers too, to craft our disasters into art.

While loss may be ordinary and pervasive in the world, it strikes us individually as exceptional and unique. Few of us are as sanguine as Bishop that art can so readily appease grief. In writing about pandemic performance, I've been less convinced that art can *master* loss than supply a crucial holding form to support us in collective grief. Theatre did so by innovating forms that straddled digital and in-person experiences to respond to its own mortality, as well as to the loss of industries, careers, social forms, and human life. In this, theatre performed functions typically associated with funeral ceremonies, health support, and social care, as these services strained under demand. The cruel irony, of course, as we saw in Section 1, is that even as it performed these critical cultural interventions, theatre was rewarded with a swathe of government cuts. While the arts should never be expected to replace health and social care, which require a different set of skills and expertise, this adaptation also usefully insisted that we saw grief not solely as a private matter that requires emotional withdrawal but as a deeply social phenomenon capable of being provoked and soothed by cultural practices and political negligence or intervention.

In *We, the Heartbroken*, Gargi Bhattacharyya goes so far as to claim that 'grief is a necessary component of a revolutionary imagination' (2023: 4). By this, Bhattacharyya suggests that grief exposes us to our interconnectedness and interdependence, pointing to the fact that the causes for our grief can only be addressed by collective action. 'Address grief as a personal wound, something to make us stronger, an opportunity to display that most dubious of attributes, resilience', Bhattacharyya cautions, 'and the tiny cracks through which collective redemption might begin to seep close up' (2023: 4). Theatre is a potent instrument of the revolutionary imagination, precisely because it understands social and cultural collectivity as a precondition to meaningful action. Grief is privatised in many western cultures because it is known to be dangerous for challenging conventions of civility and propriety, while theatre's most profound facility is to harness group feeling for collective response. Acknowledging pandemic grief may contribute to countering the logics of isolation and contagion, which regulated the period, with what Benjamin Bratton has defined as a '*positive biopolitics* on a new rationality of inclusion, care, transformation and prevention' (2022: 173), which requires not only a political response but also intervention from the arts and humanities.

If the kind of work explored here encourages us to approach grief collectively, it also helps us to perceive grief as a cross-temporal and cross-cultural phenomenon. In writing about pandemic grief, I am suggesting that the experience was both temporally, geographically, and experientially particular, but grief itself, as the appeal to tragic templates suggests, is as old as time and as uncertain as the future. History has taught us that pandemic time is never neatly contained by pre- and post-pandemic periods, but that it is always engulfed by a pool of inter-pandemic time that awaits another pandemic to strike again. In the historical references and dramaturgical frames that support the works explored in this text, including Greek and Shakespearean tragedy, theatre appears not just as a tool of the present but as a vehicle that shuttles across eras, cultures, and forms, reminding us of the losses that came before us and which will inevitably occur again. It may not be the case that this work will survive and be restaged like *The Trojan Women* or *Antigone*, but one of the aims of this text is to help document this archive of theatrical grief – to name and account for the works, as Jo Clifford and Lesley Orr did for the dead with *The Covid Requiem* – so that it might guide inevitable future losses, including those of a similar form and scale.

While I have followed a trajectory that shows theatre moving through phases of mourning, consolation, and an appetite for life, neither grief nor grief for theatre follow a linear route. It would be remiss, therefore, to end on a note that implies that the effects of the pandemic have run their course. While some parts of life have returned to the semblance of pre-pandemic normality, we still live with its resurgences, as well as the aftershocks of individual and collective grief: numerous theatre institutions have closed down or made their staff redundant; funding has been cut; attendance has dropped and has not evenly recovered; arts and humanities subjects are routinely attacked, especially by the UK's Conservative government. These conditions are compounded by hikes in energy prices and a cost of living crisis that makes theatre buildings too difficult to run, and audiences' reluctance to spend money on attending. Part of living through grief means accepting that some grief is unending.

The scale of the existential threat facing the theatre industry was captured in a *New York Times* article published in 2023, which catalogued a litany of cancelled festivals and institutions in crisis in the USA, with the author claiming that a bailout was required save the sector. This slow death of many theatres, as proposed by the article's author Isaac Butler, was 'exacerbated by the pandemic, a ruinous event that has closed theaters, broken the theatergoing habit for audiences and led to a calamitous increase in costs at a moment when they can least be absorbed' (2023).

Towards the end of his life, Donald W. Winnicott recorded a prayer in his notebook: 'Oh God! May I be alive when I die' (Winnicott in Adès 2016: 297). While I have focused on how theatre supported grief arising from pandemic death and loss, the work also carries a profound and often moving sense of aliveness in death. Even as so many venues, companies, and careers ended, at its most wounded and threatened, the form enacted and held out hope for aliveness in the face of death – a refusal to let grief drown out an appetite for life in loss.

Similarly, when Tim Crouch announced that the theatre was dead, as discussed in Section 1, he was both sounding an alarm and, via his accomplished storytelling, trying to persuade us that his claim was not entirely true. Life still buzzes among the ruins. While it is accurate that some theatre careers, institutions, and organisations died in the wake of the pandemic, the form stayed alive, adapting to help navigate the pressures and losses engendered by Covid-19.

Seven months after seeing *Truth's a Dog Must to a Kennel* at Battersea Arts Centre, I returned to the theatre for Miet Warlop's *One Song*. The seating arrangement had been expanded to accommodate a room full of twitching spectators who came to witness the production widely lauded since its premiere at the Avignon Festival in 2022.

Featuring twelve performers, the piece begins with an umpire-commentator initiating a workout with the ensemble, who turn out to also be accomplished musicians, dancers, and athletes. A ballerina plays the violin on a bar (Elisabeth Klinck), a double bassist does sit-ups under his imposing instrument (Simon Beeckaert), a drummer sprints between kits (Melvin Slabbinck), and a cheerleader skips around the stage flashing pompoms (Milan Schude).

Behind them, a small group applauds, cheers, heckles, stomps, and sways in sync, like an excitable chorus in a Greek tragedy. Vocalist Wietse Tanghe takes to a treadmill and begins to sing about grief as he runs, with varying speed and intensity, propelled by the ensemble to keep going, who propel *him* in turn, despite mounting pain and fatigue. 'Run for your life/ 'Till you die', his refrain loops; 'Grief is like a liquid/And it never goes away/ All we need is/That it finds its way'. While Sisyphus was condemned by Hades to roll a boulder up and down a hill for eternity for twice cheating death, Tanghe's repetitive gestures are directed at finding form and function for his grief.

Tanghe's lyrics urge us to unleash the grief that's inside us 'like a rock', until it starts to shift, move, disperse, and transform under the euphoria that exceeds the pain of collective movement and choral sound. The ensemble persists until the performers visibly perspire and ache, while liquid starts to spray intermittently from the rig overhead, before the cast eventually drops in exhaustion after an hour. This is a virtuosic ritual of collapse and rebirth that nods to tragedy, endurance-based performance art, and the work of Forced Entertainment (e.g. *Bloody Mess*, 2004), which demonstrates in real time performance's capacity to find joy and unity in sustained endeavour, however futile those practices might appear to the world.

Warlop's production was commissioned as the fourth part in the NTGent series Histoire(s) du Théâtre, led by Milo Rau. It was originally conceived by Warlop as a response to the death of her brother, a grief compounded for the cast by the death of one of its members, Rint Dens, in February 2023. But given its time of creation and production, it's impossible to not also see in *One Song* a comment on the grief surrounding Covid-19, when bodies strained under pressure, sickness, and loss. But here, the body is mobilised to dissolve and reroute grief, pushing it to the limits of communal endurance. Grief is allowed to flow through shared physical and artistic performance, dramaturgically channelled and aesthetically filtered, until we encounter the surprise relief and pleasure that come when we don't hold grief in but let it course into the world – as tears, as sweat, as music, as movement, as performance; until pipes split and walls shudder, as if the skies are cracking open.

I've been circling around grief and theatre in this text, exploring how they provoked and served one another during the pandemic, and sometimes collided. What I find myself ultimately trying to convey is that because theatre has always been a deep reservoir of grief, inclined to support and guide us in and through it, as it has done from ancient tragedy to pandemic performance, the threat of its institutional demise and disciplinary destruction is particularly grave. Ultimately, pandemic grief cannot only be allowed to mourn over our individual losses in private, but it must also seep through the borders of our bodies and cracks in the public sphere, demanding that we fight to save those services, institutions, communities, and art forms that are *not* dead yet. Grief requires us to live with our losses, but more importantly, it calls on us to remember, preserve, and celebrate everything that makes life worth living. To grieve in and with pandemic theatres is to hunger for More Life, for a better life; for the kind of life that can perhaps only be glimpsed in or rehearsed for through the arts.

References

Adès, R., ed. (2016). *The Collected Works of D. W. Winnicott: Volume 12, Appendices and Bibliographies*, Oxford: Oxford University Press.

Akinjirin, A. (2021). Our Hands. In *Skin Hunger*, Glasgow: Salamander Street, pp. 32–9.

Alcor, www.alcor.org. Accessed 1 November 2023.

American Psychiatric Association. (2021). APA offers tips for understanding Prolonged grief disorder, www.psychiatry.org/news-room/news-releases/apa-offers-tips-for-understanding-prolonged-grief. Accessed 1 November 2023.

American Psychiatric Association. (2022). *DSM-5-TR* (*Diagnostic and Statistical Manual of Mental Disorders*), 5th ed., Text Revision, Washington, DC: American Psychiatric Association.

Aristotle. (1907 [1895]). *The Poetics of Aristotle*, 4th ed., ed. and trans. S. H. Butcher, London: Macmillan.

Artaud, A. (1958 [1938]). *The Theatre and Its Double*, trans. Mary Caroline Richards, New York: Grove Press.

Asibong, A. (2022). *Post-Traumatic Attachments to the Eerily Moving Image: Something to Watch Over Me*, Abingdon: Routledge.

Auslander, P. (2012). Digital Liveness: A Historico-Philosophical Perspective. *PAJ: A Journal of Performance and Art*, 34 (3), 3–11.

Barthes, R. (2012 [2009]). *Mourning Diary*, trans. Richard Howard, New York: Hill and Wang.

Beckett, S. (2010 [1961]). *Happy Days*, London: Faber and Faber.

Bectu. (2020). Theatre job losses jump from 3000 to 5000 in a month, reports Bectu, https://bectu.org.uk/news/theatre-job-losses-jump-from-3000-to-5000-in-a-month-reports-bectu?s=job%20losses&f=all. Accessed 1 November 2023.

Berkowitz, B. and A. Blanco (2021). A record number of Confederate monuments fell in 2020, but hundreds still stand. Here's where. *The Washington Post*, 17 June, www.washingtonpost.com/graphics/2020/national/confederate-monuments/. Accessed 1 November 2023.

Bhattacharyya, G. (2023). *We, the Heartbroken*, London: Hajar Press.

Bishop, E. (1976). One Art. *The New Yorker*, 26 April, p. 40.

Blau, H. (2011). *Reality Principles: From the Absurd to the Virtual*, Ann Arbor: University of Michigan Press.

Bowlby, J. (1998). *Loss: Sadness and Depression*, Volume 3: Attachment and Loss, London: Pimlico.

Bratton, B. (2022). *The Revenge of the Real: Politics for a Post-Pandemic World*, London: Verso.

Brook, P. (1996 [1968]). *The Empty Space*, New York: Touchstone.

Brown, M. (2021). Jo Clifford on seeking to bring some theatrical healing with The Covid Requiem. *The National*, 5 September, www.thenational.scot/news/19559586.jo-clifford-seeking-bring-theatrical-healing-covid-requiem/. Accessed 1 November 2023.

Butler, I. (2023). American theater is imploding before our eyes. *The New York Times*, 19 July, www.nytimes.com/2023/07/19/opinion/theater-collapse-bail out.html. Accessed 1 November 2023.

Butler, J. (2009). *Frames of War: When Is Life Grievable?* London: Verso.

Butler, J. (2015). *Notes Towards a Performative Theory of Assembly*, Cambridge, MA: Harvard University Press.

Buyse, A. (2021). Pandemic Protests: Creatively Using the Freedom of Assembly during COVID-19. *Netherlands Quarterly of Human Rights*, 39 (4), 265–267.

Carlson, M. (2001). *The Haunted Stage: The Theatre as Memory Machine*, Ann Arbor: The University of Michigan Press.

Carr, M. (2006). *Woman and Scarecrow*, London: Faber and Faber.

Carson, A. (2007). Tragedy: A Curious Art Form. In *Grief Lessons: Four Plays by Euripides*, trans., Anne Carson, New York: New York Review Books, pp.7–9.

Caruth, C., ed. (1995). *Trauma: Explorations in Memory*, Baltimore: The Johns Hopkins University Press.

Chao-Fong, L. (2021). Recorded homophobic hate crimes soared in pandemic, figures show. *The Guardian*, 3 December, www.theguardian.com/world/2021/dec/03/recorded-homophobic-hate-crimes-soared-in-pandemic-figures-show. Accessed 1 November 2023.

Chillingworth, H. (2020). In conversation with Hester Chillingworth, https://royalcourttheatre.com/in-conversation-with-hester-chillingworth/. Accessed 1 November 2023.

Cholbi, M. (2021). *Grief: A Philosophical Guide*, New Jersey: Princeton University Press.

Churchill, C. (2019 [2016]). Escaped Alone. In *Churchill: Plays Five*. London: Nick Hern Books, 137–79.

Clifford, J. (2021). Jo Clifford: The falling leaves remind us of the loss of the pandemic but spring, and hope, is on its way. *The Sunday Post*, 12 September, www.sundaypost.com/fp/requiem/. Accessed 1 November 2023.

Clifford, J. and L. Orr (2021). *The Covid Requiem*. (Unpublished script of the iteration at St. Mary's Episcopal Cathedral, Edinburgh).

Cocteau, J. (1961). Orphée. *Jean Cocteau: Five Plays* [English Version by Carl Wildman], New York: Hill and Wang, pp. 1–46.

Cooper, F., L. Dolezal and A. Rose (2023). *Covid-19 and Shame: Political Emotions and Public Health in the UK*, London: Bloomsbury Academic.

Crouch, T. (2021). The Sessions. In *Skin Hunger*, Glasgow: Salamander Street, pp. 49–53.

Crouch, T. (2022). *Truth's a Dog Must to a Kennel*, London: Methuen Drama.

Dante or Die. (2021). *Skin Hunger on Film*, Dante or Die and Snow Films.

Despret, V. (2021 [2015]). *Our Grateful Dead: Stories of Those Left Behind*, trans. Stephen Muecke: University of Minnesota Press.

Didion, J. (2005). *The Year of Magical Thinking*. New York: Alfred. A. Knopf.

Doka, K., ed. (2002). *Disenfranchised Grief: New Directions, Challenges, and Strategies for Practice*, Champaign, IL: Research Press.

Ernaux, A. (2018 [2008]). *The Years*, trans. Alison L. Strayer, London: Fitzcarraldo Editions.

Euripides. (2009). *The Trojan Women*, trans. A. Shapiro, Oxford: Oxford University Press.

European Commission. (2022). *Future Brief: Covid-19 and the Environment: Links*, *Impacts and Lessons Learned*, 26 July, https://op.europa.eu/en/publi cation-detail/-/publication/d9a15ec3-1ea2-11ed-8fa0-01aa75ed71a1/lan guage-en. Accessed 1 November 2023.

Evans, A., C. ter Culle and I. Williams (2021). *This Too Shall Pass*: *Mourning Collective Loss in the Time of Covid-19*, https://larger.us/wp-content/ uploads/2021/01/This-Too-Shall-Pass.pdf. Accessed 1 November 2023.

Freud, S. and J. Breuer (2001 [1895]). Studies on Hysteria. In J. Strachey, ed. and trans., *The Standard Edition of the Complete Psychological Works of Sigmund Freud*, Volume II (1893–1895), London: Vintage.

Freud, S. (2001 [1916]). On Transience. In J. Strachey, ed. and trans., *The Standard Edition of the Complete Psychological Works of Sigmund Freud*, Volume XIV (1914–1916), London: Vintage, pp. 301–7.

Freud, S. (2001 [1917]). Mourning and Melancholia. In J. Strachey, ed. and trans., *The Standard Edition of the Complete Psychological Works of Sigmund Freud*, Volume XIV (1914–1916), London: Vintage, pp. 237–60.

Fuchs, B. (2022). *Theater of Lockdown*: *Digital and Distanced Performance in a Time of Pandemic*, London: Methuen Drama.

Giorgis, P., O. Semenets and B. Todorova (2023). 'We are at war': The military rhetoric of COVID-19 in cross-cultural perspective of discourses. *Frontiers in Artificial Intelligence*, 9 March, www.frontiersin.org/articles/10.3389/ frai.2023.978096/full. Accessed 1 November 2023.

Greenberg, N., M. Docherty, S. Gnanapragasam and S. Wessely (2020). Managing mental health challenges faced by healthcare workers during covid-19 pandemic. *The BJM*, 368 (March), www.bmj.com/content/368/ bmj.m1211?ijkey=f0b03dd6a6af903754bc0c828f01352b02119842&keyty pe2=tf_ipsecsha. Accessed 1 November 2023.

Hallett, H. (2022). UK Covid-19 inquiry opening statement, https://covid19 .public-inquiry.uk/wp-content/uploads/2022/07/UK-Covid19-Inquiry-Launch-Statement.pdf. Accessed 1 November 2023.

Harris, D. L. (2020). Introduction. In D. L. Harris, ed., *Non-death Loss and Grief: Context and Clinical Implications*, New York: Routledge, pp. 1–6.

Hartman, S. (2002). The Time of Slavery. *The South Atlantic Quarterly*, 101 (4), 757–77.

Hemley, M. (2023). West End box office and attendance up in 2022, according to first full data since Covid. *The Stage*, 13 February, www.thestage.co.uk/ news/west-end-box-office-and-attendance-up-in-2022-according-to-first-full-data-since-covid. Accessed 1 November 2023.

Hicks, D. (2020). Why Colston had to fall, *Art Review*, 9 June, https://artreview .com/why-colston-had-to-fall/. Accessed 1 November 2023.

House of Commons Health and Social Care, and Science and Technology Committees. (2021). *Coronavirus: Lessons Learned to Date Sixth Report of the Health and Social Care Committee and Third Report of the Science and Technology Committee of Session 2021–22*, https://committees.parliament.uk/ publications/7496/documents/78687/default/. Accessed 1 November 2023.

Hughes, S. (2021). Touch the Flesh. In *Skin Hunger*. Glasgow: Salamander Street, pp. 60–4.

Hyland, P., E. Redican, T. Karatzias and M. Shevlin (2023). The International Grief Questionnaire (IGQ): A new measure of ICD-11 prolonged grief disorder. *Journal of Traumatic Stress* (November), 1-13.

Jarman, D. (1993). *Blue*, Basilisk Communications.

Johnson, B. (2020). PM statement at coronavirus press conference. 5 July 2021, www.gov.uk/government/speeches/pm-statement-at-coronavirus-press-con ference-5-july-2021. Accessed 1 November 2023.

Kearney, R. (2021). *Touch: Recovering Our Most Vital Sense*, New York: Columbia University Press.

Kevorkian, K. A. (2020). Environmental grief. In D. L. Harris, ed., *Non-death Loss and Grief: Context and Clinical Implications*, New York: Routledge, pp. 216–26.

Kiong, T. C. and A. L. Schiller (1993). The Anthropology of Death: A Preliminary Overview. *Southeast Asian Journal of Social Science*, 21 (2), 1–9.

Kitson. D. (2020). *Dot.Dot.Dot.* Live stream recording accessible via the artist's website, www.danielkitson.com/. Accessed 1 November 2023.

Kübler-Ross, E. (2019 [1969]). *On Death & Dying: What the Dying Have to Teach Doctors, Nurses, Clergy & Their Own Families*, New York: Scribner.

Lieber, L. S. (2016). Stages of Grief: Enacting Lamentation in Late Ancient Hymnography. *AJS Review*, 40 (1), 101–24.

Lost Dog. (2020). *In a Nutshell.* Live stream recording accessible on YouTube, www.youtube.com/watch?v=CiMX1_bE7U8. Accessed 1 November 2023.

Marker, C., A. Resnais and C. Ghislain (1953). *Les Statues Meurent Aussi.* Présence Africaine and Tadié Cinéma.

Mathew, T. (2020). Professional Mourners' Laments from Quarantine. *The New Yorker*, 9 June, www.newyorker.com/culture/video-dept/professional-mourners-laments-from-quarantine. Accessed 1 November 2023.

Mitima-Verloopa, H. B., T. T. M. Moorena and P. A. Boelena (2021). Facilitating Grief: An Exploration of the Function of Funerals and Rituals in Relation to Grief Reactions. *Death Studies*, 45 (9), 735–45.

Movement Advancement Project. (2020). *The Rise of Hate Crimes.* 29 May, https://lgbtmap.medium.com/education-action-during-covid-19-the-rise-of-hate-crimes-a261fd723c8a. Accessed 1 November 2023.

Neimeyer, R. A. and B. E. Thompson (2014). Meaning Making and the Art of Grief Therapy. In B. E. Thompson and R. A. Neimeyer, eds., *Grief and the Expressive Arts*. New York: Routledge, pp. 3–13.

O'Callaghan, C. C., F. McDermott, P. Hudson and J. R. Zalcberg (2013). Sound Continuing Bonds with the Deceased: The Relevance of Music, Including Preloss Music Therapy, for Eight Bereaved Caregivers. *Death Studies*, 37(2), 101–25.

O'Connell, M. (2017). *To Be a Machine: Adventures among Cyborgs, Utopians, Hackers, and the Futurists Solving the Modest Problem of Death*, London: Granta.

O'Farrell, M. (2020). *Hamnet.* London: Tinder Press.

Ofcom. (2020). *Online Nation: 2020 Summary Report*, www.ofcom.org.uk/__data/assets/pdf_file/0028/196408/online-nation-2020-summary.pdf. Accessed 1 November 2023.

Office for National Statistics. (2020). *Coronavirus and Key Workers in the UK*, www.ons.gov.uk/employmentandlabourmarket/peopleinwork/earningsand workinghours/articles/coronavirusandkeyworkersintheuk/2020-05-15. Accessed 1 November 2023.

Office for National Statistics. (2020a). *Coronavirus (COVID-19) Related Deaths by Ethnic Group, England and Wales: 2 March 2020 to 10 April 2020*, www .ons.gov.uk/peoplepopulationandcommunity/birthsdeathsandmarriages/

deaths/articles/coronavirusrelateddeathsbyethnicgroupenglandandwales/
2march2020to10april2020. Accessed 1 November 2023.

Office for National Statistics. (2023). Deaths involving coronavirus (COVID-19), www.ons.gov.uk/peoplepopulationandcommunity/healthandsocialcare/condi tionsanddiseases/articles/coronaviruscovid19latestinsights/deaths#:~: text=Deaths%20involving%20COVID%2D19%20were%20highest%20for %20those%20aged%2085,in%20the%20oldest%20age%20groups. Accessed 1 November 2023.

Office for Students. (2021). OfS confirms funding reforms, www.officeforstu dents.org.uk/news-blog-and-events/press-and-media/ofs-confirms-funding-reforms/. Accessed 1 November 2023.

Oprysko, C. and S. Luthi (2020). Trump labels himself 'a wartime president' combating coronavirus. *Politico*, 18 March, www.politico.com/news/2020/ 03/18/trump-administration-self-swab-coronavirus-tests-135590. Accessed 1 November 2023.

Owen, L. and M. Zaroulia (2022). Re-membering assembly. In C. Wallace, C. Escoda, E. Monforte and J. R. Prado-Pérez, eds., *Crisis, Representation and Resilience: Perspectives on Contemporary British Theatre*, London: Methuen Drama, pp. 209–25.

Phelan, P. (1993). *Mourning Sex: Performing Public Memories*, Abingdon: Routledge.

Pierce, M., H. Hope, T. Ford, S. Hatch, M. Hotopf, A. John et al. (2020). Mental Health Before and during the COVID-19 Pandemic: A Longitudinal Probability Sample Survey of the UK Population. *Lancet Psychiatry*, 7, 883–92.

Police, Crime, Sentencing and Courts Act. (2022. www.legislation.gov.uk/ ukpga/2022/32/contents/enacted. Accessed 1 November 2023.

Porter, M. (2015). *Grief Is the Thing with Feathers*, London: Faber & Faber.

Press Association (2023). Arts Council warns of 'worrying' decline in young people attending events, www.irishtimes.com/ireland/2023/07/23/arts-coun cil-warns-of-worrying-decline-in-young-people-attending-events/. Accessed 1 November 2023.

Public Order Act. (2023). www.legislation.gov.uk/ukpga/2023/15/enacted. Accessed 1 November 2023.

Quashie, K. (2021). *Black Aliveness, or a Poetics of Being*, Durham: Duke University Press.

Raleigh, V. (2022). Deaths from Covid-19 (coronavirus): How are they counted and what do they show? 23 August, www.kingsfund.org.uk/publications/deaths-covid-19?gclid=Cj0KCQjw2eilBhCCARIsAG0Pf8thyXwADWgaFIeGDupGq 0zD_a07UaNdjr1XnZHWDXJYZwLq-DRIDKsaAgh8EALw_wcB. Accessed 1 November 2023.

Rando, T. A. (1984). *Grief, Dying, and Death: Clinical Interventions for Caregivers*, Champaign, IL: Research Press Company.

Rankine, C. (2015). The Condition of Black Life Is One of Mourning. *The New York Times Magazine*, www.nytimes.com/2015/06/22/magazine/the-con dition-of-black-life-is-one-of-mourning.html. Accessed 1 November 2023.

Ravenhill, M. (2011). *Ten Plagues* [and *The Coronation of* Poppea], London: Methuen Drama.

Rivers, W. H. R. (1913). The Contact of Peoples. In E. C. Quiggin, ed., *Essays and Studies Presented to William Ridgeway*, Cambridge: Cambridge University Press, pp. 474–92.

Rose, J. (2023). *The Plague*, London: Fitzcarraldo Editions.

Roy, D. J. (2001). That All Not Be Lost. *Journal of Palliative Care*, 17 (3), 131–2.

Shakespeare, W. (1992). *Hamlet*, New York: Dover.

Shakespeare, W. (2015). *King Lear*, eds. B. A. Mowat and P. Werstine, New York: Simon & Schuster.

Sharpe, C. (2016). *In the Wake: On Blackness and Being*, Durham: Duke University Press.

Simon, T. (2020). *An Occupation of Loss: Laments from Quarantine*. Films accessible via Artangel's website, www.artangel.org.uk/an-occupation-of-loss/laments-from-quarantine/. Accessed 1 November 2023.

Sophocles. (1984). *The Three Theban Plays: 'Antigone', 'Oedipus the King', 'Oedipus at Colonus'*, trans. R. Fagles, London: Penguin Books.

Stein, A. (2004). Music, Mourning, and Consolation. *Journal of the American Psychoanalytic Association*, 52, 783–811.

Stroebe, M. and H. Schut (1999). The Dual Process Model of Coping with Bereavement: Rationale and Description. *Death Studies*, 23 (3), 197–224.

Sudbury-Riley, L. and B. Giordano (2021). *The Lived Experiences of People Bereaved by Covid-19*, www.liverpool.ac.uk/management/research/ impact/the-lived-experiences-of-people-bereaved-by-covid-19/. Accessed 1 November 2023.

Talawa Theatre. (2020–1). *Tales from the Front Line . . . and Other Stories* (2020-1). Films accessible via the company's website, www.talawa.com/productions/tales-from-the-front-line and on YouTube, www.youtube.com/playlist?list=PLbdL1-fPId8PPfwnUwadnqpbKbn4P2WPo. Accessed 1 November 2023.

The Health Foundation. (2020). Black and minority ethnic workers make up a disproportionately large share of key worker sectors in London, 7 May, www.health.org.uk/black-and-minority-ethnic-workers-make-up-a-dispro portionately-large-share-of-key-worker-sectors-in. Accessed 1 November 2023.

The Lancet Editorial. (2020). The plight of essential workers during the COVID-19 pandemic. *The Lancet*, 395 (10237), 23 May, www.thelancet .com/journals/lancet/article/PIIS0140-6736(20)31200-9/fulltext. Accessed 1 November 2023.

Varadkar, L. (2020). Statement by An Taoiseach Leo Varadkar On measures to tackle Covid-19 Washington, 12 March, https://merrionstreet.ie/en/news-room/news/statement_by_an_taoiseach_leo_varadkar_on_measures_to_ tackle_covid-19_washington_12_march_2020.html. Accessed 1 November 2023.

Verlander, F. (2022). Touch (Sk)Interrupted? *Performance Research*, 27 (2), 7–15.

Von Mohr, M., L. P. Kirsch and A. Fotopoulou (2021). Social Touch Deprivation during COVID-19: Effects on Psychological Wellbeing and Craving Interpersonal Touch. *Royal Society Open Science*, 8, 1–17, www .ncbi.nlm.nih.gov/pmc/articles/PMC8424338/pdf/rsos.210287.pdf. Accessed 1 November 2023.

Walsh, F. (2021). Grief Machines: Transhumanist Theatre, Digital Performance, Pandemic Time. *Theatre Journal*, 73 (3), 391–407.

Walsh, F. (2023). *Performing the Queer Past: Public Possessions*, London: Methuen.

Weaver, M. (2023). 'Nature's way of dealing with old people': The damning messages revealed to Covid inquiry. *The Guardian*, 31 October, www.theguar dian.com/uk-news/2023/oct/31/natures-way-of-dealing-with-old-people-the-damning-messages-revealed-to-covid-inquiry. Accessed 1 November 2023.

Wilson, E. R. (2004). *Mocked with Death: Tragic Overliving from Sophocles to Milton*, Baltimore: The Johns Hopkins University Press.

Winnicott, D. W. (1975 [1951]). *Through Paediatrics to Psycho-Analysis*, New York: Basic Books.

Winnicott, D. W. (2005 [1971]). *Playing and Reality*, Abingdon: Routledge Classics.

Wojnarowicz, D. (1999). *In the Shadow of the American Dream: The Diaries of David Wojnarowicz* New York: Grove Press.

Woodthorpe, K. and H. Rumble (2022). 'My Memories of the Time We Had Together Are More Important': Direct Cremation and the Privatisation of UK Funerals. *Sociology*, 56 (3), 556–73.

Acknowledgements

Some of the ideas presented here were enriched by the Wellcome Trust ISSF-supported symposium Performing Pandemic Grief: The Arts of Losing, held at Birkbeck Centre for Contemporary Theatre in November 2022. I'm grateful to the funder and to all those who contributed to the conference, especially Louise Owen and Jack McIntosh who helped organise the event. Thanks to Ramona Mosse and Nina Tecklenburg who invited me to speak on the subject at the Viral Theatres: Pandemic Past/Hybrid Futures symposium at the Tieranatomisches Theater Berlin in 2022. My Contemporary Performance Texts and Cambridge University Press editorial colleagues supported the preparation of the manuscript, in particular Emily Hockley, Duška Radosavljević, and Caridad Svich. I'm also thankful to the theatre makers who provided me with access to the resources that are referenced and reproduced in this Element, in particular Stuart Armitt, Hester Stefan Chillingworth, Jo Clifford, Tim Crouch, Lesley Orr, and Phillip McMahon. Two peer reviewers offered feedback that benefitted the text, and for this I am also grateful. Students have never been far from my mind during this project. They helped me make sense of the changes taking place to theatre during the pandemic period, even as they confronted the pressures of new teaching and learning arrangements, and an existential threat to the discipline they so passionately invested in. I thank them for the patience, commitment, and optimism that buoyed us all up as so much else seemed to fall.

Finally, I'm indebted to all those friends whose messages, calls, FaceTimes, and promises of meeting again made the pandemic experience less arduous than it could have been, including Áine Brocklebank, Fiona Collins, David Cregan, Nadia Davids, Joseph Gubbins, Barry Johnston, Graham Little, Brian Martin, Phillip McMahon, Aoife Monks, Louise Owen, Willy Papa, George Pearse, Thomas Rogers, and Luigi Di Venere. I loved you on-screen but prefer you in *real life*.

for
Louise, Luigi, Phillip, Thomas and Willy

About the Author

Fintan Walsh is Professor of Performing Arts and Humanities at Birkbeck, University of London, where he is Head of the School of Creative Arts, Culture and Communication and Director of Birkbeck Centre for Contemporary Theatre. His most recent book is *Performing the Queer Past: Public Possessions* (Methuen Drama, 2023). Fintan is a former Senior Editor of the journal *Theatre Research International* and is founding Senior Editor of the Cambridge University Press series Elements in Contemporary Performance Texts.

Cambridge Elements ≡

Contemporary Performance Texts

Senior Editor
Fintan Walsh
Birkbeck, University of London

Fintan Walsh is Professor of Performing Arts and Humanities at Birkbeck, University of London, where he is Head of the School of Creative Arts, Culture and Communication and Director of Birkbeck Centre for Contemporary Theatre. He is a former Senior Editor of *Theatre Research International*.

Associate Editors
Duška Radosavljević
Royal Central School of Speech and Drama, University of London

Duška Radosavljević is a Professorial Research Fellow at the Royal Central School of Speech and Drama. Her work has received the David Bradby Research Prize (2015), the Elliott Hayes Award for Dramaturgy (2022) and the ATHE-ASTR Award for Digital Scholarship.

Caridad Svich
Rutgers University

Caridad Svich is a playwright and translator. She teaches creative writing and playwriting in the English Department at Rutgers University-New Brunswick.

Advisory Board
Siân Adiseshiah, *Loughborough University*
Helena Grehan, *Western Australian Academy of Performing Arts*
Ameet Parameswaran, *Jawaharlal Nehru University*
Synne Behrndt, *Stockholm University of the Arts*
Jay Pather, *University of Cape Town*
Sodja Zupanc Lotker, *The Academy of Performing Arts in Prague (DAMU)*
Peter M. Boenisch, *Aarhus University*
Hayato Kosuge, *Keio University*
Edward Ziter, *NYU Tisch School of the Arts*
Milena Gras Kleiner, *Pontificia Universidad Católica de Chile*
Savas Patsalidis, *Aristotle University, Thessaloniki, Greece*
Harvey Young, *College of Fine Arts, Boston University*

About the Series
Contemporary Performance Texts responds to the evolution of the form, role and meaning of text in theatre and performance in the late twentieth and twenty-first centuries, by publishing Elements that explore the generation of text for performance, its uses in performance, and its varied modes of reception and documentation.

Cambridge Elements ⁼

Contemporary Performance Texts

Elements in the Series

Playwriting, Dramaturgy and Space
Sara Freeman

Performing Grief in Pandemic Theatres
Fintan Walsh

A full series listing is available at: www.cambridge.org/ECTX

Printed in the United States
by Baker & Taylor Publisher Services